21
DAYS
TO SUCCESS
With
LINKEDIN

What People Are Saying About *21 Days to Success With LinkedIn*

"I love how you sum everything up in the Aha! moments. And quite frankly, now I feel like LinkedIn is an effective way to network, where I really didn't understand the point of it before."

—Katelyn Dalton, college student

"Very thorough. Having recently completed a live LinkedIn training course taught by one of the world's largest outplacement firms, I am impressed by the detail and organization of *21 Days to Success With LinkedIn*. It's convinced me to make it a habit!"

—Craig Freeze, healthcare account executive

"The lessons I learned have really helped me create more positive, professional relationships on LinkedIn."

—Matt O'Malley, insurance agent

"After a speedy start reading *21 Days to Success With LinkedIn*, it has been 12 days and I am still absorbing it. In fact, I find I truly am on Day 12. It's not a mystery novel, though it does solve some mysteries for me and is hard to put down. Read it with your LinkedIn access (PC, laptop, mobile phone) close by, because you'll want to try it along with Gnik, as I have done. You will see it come to life before your eyes."

—Rich Tensmeyer, QA specialist

"After reading *21 Days*, I am reminded of the age-old question of the best way to eat an elephant—one bite at a time. Well, now I feel more confident how to develop my presence on LinkedIn—one *day* at a time."

—Carl Seyerle, (airport) ramp agent

Business Social Networking the Gnik Rowten Way

Ron Sukenick and Ken Williams

Information Today, Inc.
Medford, New Jersey

First Printing, 2015

21 Days to Success With LinkedIn: Business Social Networking the Gnik Rowten Way

Library of Congress Cataloging-in-Publication Data

Sukenick, Ron, author.
21 days to success with LinkedIn : business social networking the Gnik Rowten way / by Ron Sukenick and Ken Williams.
pages cm
ISBN 978-1-937290-05-4
1. LinkedIn (Electronic resource) 2. Business networks. 3. Social interaction. I. Williams, Ken, 1968– author. II. Title. III. Title: Twenty one days to success with LinkedIn.
HD69.S8S8496 2016
650.140285'6754—dc23

2015031747

Printed and bound in the United States of America.

President and CEO: Thomas H. Hogan, Sr.
Editor-in-Chief and Publisher: John B. Bryans
Production Manager: Tiffany Chamenko
Project Editor: Jim Waltzer
Cover Designers: Lisa Conroy, Denise Erickson

Images of Gnik, Pam, and Garrett created by Kim Sharpe (facebook.com/kimmortal1)

Typesetting by Amnet Systems

infotoday.com

To everyone who has supported the
travels and adventures of Gnik.
Your enthusiasm has allowed his life to
move in new directions.

Contents

Authors' Note

Our first book together, *21 Days to Success Through Networking*, is a dynamic business allegory that teaches both basic and advanced principles of face-to-face networking through the experiences of a fictional character, Gnik Rowten (that's "networking" spelled backwards). Over a three-week period, Gnik (pronounced "Nick") embarks on an adventure that takes him out of his comfort zone and, ultimately, equips him with the necessary skills to develop a great personal network.

A few of Gnik's mentors from the earlier book return in *21 Days to Success With LinkedIn* to help him implement specific strategies and techniques for success on LinkedIn. Although it is not necessary to read *21 Days to Success Through Networking* to benefit from the new book, the principles discussed in the books are complementary.

LinkedIn is an evolving business networking tool, and we have made every effort to reflect current and accurate information about what we consider its most powerful features. Many tips and techniques are presented in our story, but specific step-by-step instructions typically are not. While the general principles are durable, the individual point-and-click steps will continue to evolve.

The primary emphasis of this book is to discuss the most commonly used and widely available features of LinkedIn, which can be accessed with a basic (free) account. However, we want to emphasize that there are a variety of premium subscription options designed to broaden your reach, increase your visibility, and deliver more targeted search results, among other benefits. Once you've gotten the hang of basic LinkedIn, you owe it to yourself to study the options and consider "graduating" to a premium account.

We hope you enjoy taking this new three-week journey with Gnik, his mentor Pam, and Garrett, who first introduced Gnik to the power of LinkedIn.

Ron Sukenick
Ken Williams
September 2015

Acknowledgments

Ron Sukenick and I teamed up a couple of years ago to write a book about networking. His concept was to create a story that would teach people how to become better networkers. With the support of friends, family, and the team at Information Today, Inc., we put together *21 Days to Success Through Networking* in 2012.

The story struck a chord—we regularly hear from readers about the impact it's had on their networking success. Believing that related subjects could be examined in like fashion, we went back to Information Today's Editor-in-Chief John B. Bryans to seek a new adventure for the redoubtable Gnik.

"Can you have Gnik learn to use LinkedIn?" John asked, and our next tale was born. Like Gnik, I had joined LinkedIn but was not a frequent user. I loved the idea of a LinkedIn tutorial, but had no idea where to start.

Ron reached out to several people who have made LinkedIn a substantial part of their business identity; without their kindness and insight, this book wouldn't have gotten off the drawing board. You will meet them during the course of our story. We are grateful to (in order of their appearance in the book) Victoria Ipri, Donna Serdula, Matt Scherer, Jason Alba, JD Gershbein, Wayne Breitbarth, Ted Prodromou, Phil Gerbyshak, Mike O'Neil, Viveka Von Rosen, and Melonie Dodaro. They are all real people, who give Gnik critical support and advice within these pages.

Others supported the project in different ways. We thank those who read early copies of the manuscript and provided feedback, especially Jan Grambo. Not only did she spot typos and missing words with eagle eyes, but her thoughtful reading identified explanations that could be improved, clarifying Gnik's LinkedIn journey. Scott Brown, Charlene Burke, and Jim Waltzer brought additional, valuable knowledge and skill to the manuscript.

Finally, both Ron and I have amazing families whose understanding enabled us to complete this project. Thank you, Yvonne, Christine, and Freedom; Marcene, Allison (and Justin!), Brendan, Carissa, Dallton, and Eddison. Thank you for letting our lives revolve around LinkedIn for awhile, and for listening to our shared excitement as we explored this new land—a couple of Gniks in the flesh.

Ken Williams

Prologue

Gnik tightened the seatbelt and glanced at his watch. *10:27 PM*. He reread the text he'd composed:

> Hey, Pam—it's me again. Gnik with a "G." Do you have some time to chat tomorrow morning? Regular time, regular place? Let me know.

Satisfied, he pressed the send button on his phone just as the flight attendant made the announcement to turn off all electronic devices. He complied, tucking his phone into the breast pocket of his sport coat. He looked absently at the safety instruction card as his mind replayed the presentation he'd given a few short hours earlier.

"Business or pleasure?" The woman interrupting his thoughts looked the part of a seasoned traveler.

"A little of both, I guess," Gnik said. "I spent the weekend back home visiting friends and family, but I was also able to squeeze in a marketing presentation."

The woman produced a book of crossword puzzles and flipped to one she'd partially completed. She held the page open with her finger before turning back to Gnik. "You're interested in marketing?"

"I launched my own marketing firm just over a year ago."

Gnik was tired from a busy weekend, but he recognized this as an opportunity to make a new connection with a fellow traveler. The two exchanged names—she introduced herself as Whitney—and Gnik turned the conversation to his seatmate. "What about you, Whitney? What do you do?"

She put a pencil in her book and closed the pages around it. With a wry smile, she said, "You wouldn't believe me."

Gnik realized he was enjoying the banter. His smile was a challenge. "Try me."

She laughed. "I'm a stand-up comedian."

"*Really*? Tell me about that. I don't think I've ever met a stand-up comedian outside of a comedy club."

Whitney spoke for several minutes about her gigs, the people she'd met, and the challenges of her chosen career.

Gnik again thought of the presentation he'd given just a few hours earlier. The feedback he'd received included a suggestion to relax his speech. He shared this with Whitney, then added, "Maybe I can help with some of your marketing, and you can give me some tips on how to be more entertaining. Do you have a card?"

She looked through her purse but came up empty. "I must have packed them in my suitcase. Are you on LinkedIn? You can find me there."

Gnik's thoughts raced back to a conversation he'd had about LinkedIn with Garrett, who'd been part of his informal "planning group." Garrett had recommended the online service as part of Gnik's networking strategy. While Gnik had gone so far as to set up an account and connect with a few friends and business contacts, he'd yet to delve any deeper than that.

"I *am* on LinkedIn," Gnik said to Whitney, "but I'm pretty new to it. How do I find you?"

"Simple. Just type my name in the search box on your homepage." She made sure he wrote down her full name and email address, and they agreed to keep in touch.

As Whitney went back to work on her crossword puzzles, Gnik leaned back and considered his past LinkedIn strategy.

What strategy? he thought ruefully.

He made some notes on his to-do list. "Meet with Pam," and, at the top of the list, "Reconnect with Garrett!"

day 1

I'm on LinkedIn. Now What?

Gnik reviewed his calendar first thing in the morning. "Nothing so pressing that I can't move it around," he mused. Feeling an urgency to meet with Garrett, he scrolled through his mobile contacts until he found the number then pressed the phone icon. *I suppose I could have texted him,* he thought as the call went through, *but nothing beats the personal touch.*

Garrett answered on the third ring.

"Garrett? Good morning—it's Gnik Rowten ... Gnik with a 'G,' remember?"

"Of course I remember you, Gnik. You were just starting your marketing business when we last met, if I recall correctly."

"You've got a good memory," Gnik said, smiling. "I know you must be busy, but I have a couple of questions if you can spare a few minutes."

He could hear papers rustling, then Garrett said, "Actually, I have about 10 minutes right now, Gnik. What's on your mind?"

Gnik had a *lot* on his mind. "When we met, you talked about taking some of my networking interactions online and specifically recommended LinkedIn. After that conversation, I set up an account and connected with a few friends—mostly my college crew and a few business contacts here in the city. But something I heard yesterday got me thinking there must be opportunities to use LinkedIn in ways I hadn't even considered. I'm looking for some direction and I thought of you right away—after all, you were the one who told me I can never have too many friends."

Garrett chuckled. "Actually, Gnik, you have 'friends' on Facebook, but on LinkedIn, they're 'connections.' There's a lot to LinkedIn. In fact, there's far too much to fit into the 10 minutes we have right now, so let me leave you with a few questions. Think about them, and we can schedule a time to talk in a couple of days."

Gnik flinched. Garrett asked great, insightful questions, but they tended to make you think harder and deeper than you were prepared to do.

"Shoot." Gnik's outward confidence hid his apprehension.

"Let's start with the basics. Don't answer me right now, just jot the questions down and we'll discuss them later. First, do you have an All-Star profile?"

Garrett paused while Gnik made a note of it. "Got it," Gnik said.

"Next, how are you going to use LinkedIn? As a way to stay in touch with business contacts? To find a job? Or are you trying to find clients and customers?"

"Okay, I need to think about that."

"And one more question for now: Who is your coach?"

"Coach?"

Garrett hesitated, then said, "I'm going to leave it at that for now. You can interpret the questions however you want. Let's talk in a few days."

How are you going to use LinkedIn? For you, is it going to be a way to stay in touch with business contacts, are you looking for a job, or are you trying to find clients and customers?

After they hung up, Gnik considered the questions as he peeled a banana at his kitchen table. He suspected they had multiple levels of meaning. When he turned on his laptop and looked at his LinkedIn profile for the first time in months, he felt an immediate twinge of embarrassment. As a marketing expert, he knew it should effectively represent his personal and professional brand. What he was looking at came up well short in that department.

"I have to enhance this profile to reflect who I am and what I have to offer."

He'd almost said it out loud. The thought bounced around his head as he picked up his smartphone and checked for new text messages. If Pam was available for a meeting, he would need to

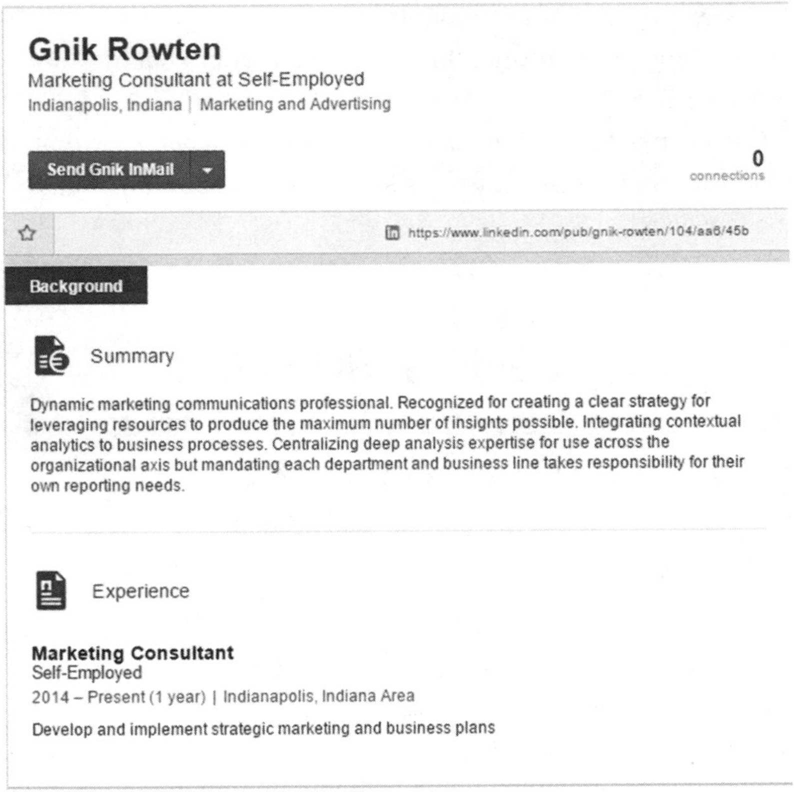

Gnik Rowten
Marketing Consultant at Self-Employed
Indianapolis, Indiana | Marketing and Advertising

Send Gnik InMail

0
connections

https://www.linkedin.com/pub/gnik-rowten/104/aa6/45b

Background

Summary

Dynamic marketing communications professional. Recognized for creating a clear strategy for leveraging resources to produce the maximum number of insights possible. Integrating contextual analytics to business processes. Centralizing deep analysis expertise for use across the organizational axis but mandating each department and business line takes responsibility for their own reporting needs.

Experience

Marketing Consultant
Self-Employed
2014 – Present (1 year) | Indianapolis, Indiana Area

Develop and implement strategic marketing and business plans

leave soon to get to the coffee shop at the regular time. There was a text from her, which read:

> Welcome back, Gnik! I'd love to hear about your trip and the conference. Regular time and place works for me. See you then!

Gnik quickly packed his new tablet device, a notebook and pen, and a few other items before hurrying out the door and down the street to the coffee shop. He arrived a few minutes before the appointed time, claimed the table in the corner where he and Pam typically met, and ordered his usual. Turning on the tablet, he opened his LinkedIn profile page again and stared at it, uncertain where to start.

"Hey, Gnik!" Pam's enthusiasm was always contagious. "What's going on?"

"I had to see you, Pam," he said as she ordered coffee. The two spent a few minutes catching up before she asked, "How was your presentation?"

"It went okay, but it's what happened *after* the conference that I want to talk about."

He recounted his conversation with Whitney on the plane, and how he'd decided to focus on LinkedIn to strengthen his business. He handed his tablet to Pam, then confessed, "I'm looking at my profile with new eyes, and I have to admit it's a little embarrassing."

She scrolled down the page to view the layout. "It does look a little bland," she said with a wink. "What are you going to do about it?"

"I don't even know where to start."

She let him stew in his thoughts for a moment. "Gnik, what *is* LinkedIn?" she asked finally, handing his tablet back.

He scoffed at the question. "It's a professional networking platform, of course."

"That's not what I mean," she pressed him. "What is LinkedIn to *you*?"

He leaned back in his chair and looked up at the ceiling, not at all sure what she was driving at.

"It's not a trick question, Gnik. I mean, consider that laptop I always see you with. If I were to ask what it is, you could tell me it's a computer, or you could say it's a tool for helping you develop and implement marketing strategies, or you might even call it a miniature movie theater. So, what's LinkedIn? And don't give me a technical definition—I want to know what *you* think it is and what you're going to use it for."

He leaned forward and laughed. "I have no idea!"

"Not true," she insisted. "After all, you did say you wanted to focus on it to increase your business. Just think for a minute ... what is LinkedIn to *you*?"

He pondered the question, then offered, "It's a way for people who may or may not know me to gain access to me, my services, and my network."

Pam smiled. "Very thoughtful answer. I suggest you keep that in mind as you build your profile."

Gnik realized the significance of what they'd just shared. "Thanks, Pam," he said with sincerity. "You always give me such great insights."

She shook off the compliment. "It was all you, Gnik."

They finished their coffee and she gave him a hug before heading to the door.

"Keep in touch—I want to see how this works out for you," she said.

"Absolutely. Let's talk again soon."

Gnik's Aha!

Day 1: It takes more than just signing up for LinkedIn to be "linked in." I will need to learn LinkedIn and use it effectively if I expect it to pay dividends.

day 2

First Things First—Complete Your Profile

The start of the morning was uneventful. Gnik showered and dressed for the day. Instead of heading right to the coffee shop, he dropped into the overstuffed leather chair in the middle of the room. This was his "thinking chair," and he called the room his "work room," though there wasn't a lot of space for him to work in. Somehow, sitting in the thinking chair's soft folds of leather always seemed to help him assess the day's challenges and even find solutions.

As he settled comfortably in the chair, he checked his handwritten notes from the phone conversation with Garrett and reflected on his talk with Pam. He added her now-familiar question to the three posed by Garrett.

What *is* LinkedIn?

Jotting down the answer he'd given Pam next to the question helped him focus his thoughts. *It's a way for people who may or may not know me to be able to gain access to me, my services, and my network.*

"Yeah, I kind of like that," he said aloud.

He looked at Garrett's questions and considered how he was going to use LinkedIn. It should help me to connect with others *and* others to connect with me—a two-way street. I want to use the site to increase the number of people I can help, in addition to finding people who are willing to help me.

Understanding your expectations for LinkedIn will determine how you use it.

Garrett's first question began to weigh more heavily on Gnik's mind. *Do I have an All-Star profile?* Turning on his laptop and opening his LinkedIn profile page, he noted that a "strength meter" on LinkedIn graded his profile as "Intermediate." Reviewing the sections that could be added to his profile, he wondered how much would be *too* much. Certifications? Interests? Volunteerism?

What does it take to have an All-Star profile?

Gnik reclined in his chair. *At first I thought this was a much simpler question than Garrett usually asks, but there's more to it than meets the eye.*

Experimenting, he replaced the word "All-Star" with "finished," leaned back again, and stared at the ceiling, which offered no help. *Of course it's not finished. I don't know that it'll ever be.*

He turned back to his laptop and clicked on the link to edit the "details" on his profile page. He suddenly saw the profile in a new light. *This almost looks like a resume.* He attacked the missing sections with renewed vigor. *I'm going to focus on the areas I think are the most important.*

He started with the "Experience" section. Drawing from his resume, he described past positions and his current business. He added his college degree and other education details, then listed the marketing skills he had developed.

For the "Summary" section he wrote a few sentences explaining what he could offer to potential clients. He scrolled up the page and checked that his current location and industry were correct. Just below his name, he added a brief headline that highlighted his primary skills and included his personal tagline, "Making the Most of Your Marketing Dollar."

Gnik saved the newly updated profile page and read it as if with a fresh pair of eyes. *Not perfect, but getting there.* He rechecked the profile strength meter. Simply by adding details from his resume and embellishing a bit, he had raised his profile to "Expert." *Not All-Star yet, but closer.*

He crossed off Garrett's opening question and closed his laptop, feeling that the day was off to a good start. Thinking he'd return to Garrett's other questions later, he prepared for an afternoon out of the apartment. A new client needed some copywriting, and the local library would provide the necessary resources in a distraction-free environment.

After arriving at the library, Gnik worked for several hours on the first draft of the pamphlet his client had requested. Finally satisfied with the mock-up, he emailed it to his client then read the handful of emails that had arrived since midday. There was nothing urgent, and he was ready for a refreshing walk home in the cool evening air. He left the library and followed the familiar route.

As he walked, Gnik replayed the events of the morning. The cold, clear air seemed to crystallize his thoughts as he mentally reviewed the list of questions from Garrett and Pam.

I'm on the right track, he told himself as he walked. *I have a pretty good idea how I'm going to use LinkedIn.*

He reflected on his new profile page. *It may still be a little vanilla, but so am I.* He smiled at his self-deprecating joke and immediately thought of the stand-up comedian he'd met on the plane. *I need to reach out to Whitney.*

Back home, Gnik streamed some music as he prepared his evening meal. After peeling a few potatoes, he took a seat at his computer. He typed in Whitney's information, found her LinkedIn profile, and was about to send a message.

I'm not sure she'll remember my name. Maybe I'll include a reminder ...

He tweaked LinkedIn's default connection message with some wording of his own.

> Whitney, let's strike a bargain. I help you with marketing, and you help me inject some humor into my presentations.
>
> Thanks,
> Gnik with a "G"

Finishing his meal, Gnik reviewed the day in its entirety. Remembering how tentative he had felt initially, he smiled as he realized the progress he'd made.

Gnik's Aha!

My profile may never be "perfect," but I should make it as complete as possible.

day 3

Know Your Purpose on LinkedIn

Gnik woke before his alarm had a chance to ring. He lay in the early morning shadows and gazed at the ceiling, mentally reviewing yesterday's progress. He was excited about his LinkedIn profile now, and was looking forward to the next steps he could take to build his brand.

Pam ran a limousine service and frequently drove for wedding parties, and he knew she had a good connection with a photographer. He needed a professional headshot and had reached out to her the night before. She was happy to give him the photographer's contact information.

Gnik's call to Dave the photographer went right to voicemail and he left a message. He showered and put on his favorite suit. Hopefully he'd be able to schedule some time with Dave later in the day.

Sipping his breakfast smoothie, he scanned the to-do list on his computer screen. He had just started to arrange the day's schedule when the telephone interrupted his planning. Expecting a callback from Dave, Gnik answered the phone without looking at the ID. "Hello, this is Gnik."

The familiar voice on the other end surprised him.

"Good morning, Gnik with a 'G.' Garrett here. I had a notification this morning that you'd updated your LinkedIn profile, and I took a look. Nice improvement. I wanted to touch base and see how things are going."

Gnik smiled with satisfaction. "Things are good, Garrett. Your questions really got me thinking, especially the one about an All-Star profile, and I'm getting my act together. I'm hoping to have a profile photo taken today."

"Excellent. A professional-looking headshot on your page can do a world of good." Garrett chuckled. "I can't tell you how many times I've gone to someone's profile only to see a picture of their dog. If I wanted to do business with their dog, that would be fine ... but I digress. What about the other questions?"

Gnik panicked momentarily as he tried to remember them—he knew there were two more. "I'm getting there," he replied weakly, hoping Garrett would let it go at that.

"Getting there? That doesn't sound too convincing, Gnik. Tell me more."

"Well, I began by updating my profile. At first I just filled in the gaps, but then I realized it should be a better reflection of who I am. It's not All-Star level yet, but I'm getting closer."

Garrett waited for Gnik to continue.

"And I realize that a coach can help me have better success on LinkedIn. There's a lot to learn, and trying to navigate it all myself is a tall order."

"Go on," Garrett prompted.

"I'm afraid I don't remember the other question," Gnik confessed.

"How are you going to use LinkedIn?"

It was a similar question to the one Pam had posed, and Gnik offered the same response. "I see LinkedIn as a way for people who may or may not know me to gain access to me, my services, and my network."

Garrett took a deep breath. "That's fine, Gnik, but it doesn't answer my question. Does it?"

He had a point. "I guess not," Gnik said sheepishly.

"Give it some more thought," Garrett said. "I think it's important for you to decide how you are going to use LinkedIn before you go any further." He paused for effect. "Let's talk later in the week. I'll be interested to hear what you discover."

After wrapping up the call, Gnik sat back in his chair. He had a different perspective on his early morning enthusiasm. Having a good profile is a start, he realized, but it's *only* a start.

While he was reflecting on this, Dave the photographer called and they scheduled a photo session for that afternoon. In the meantime, Gnik worked on a client project and answered his email. Scrolling through the subject lines, he looked to see if anything interesting had hit his inbox but nothing noteworthy had come in all morning.

He realized he had expected his shiny new profile to get people flocking to his LinkedIn page, and was a little surprised to see no boost in activity. Reminding himself that it had only been a few hours didn't lessen his disappointment. The line from a movie he'd seen long ago kept running through his mind. *If you build it, they will come.*

Well, he *had* built it, and would *keep* building it, but he told himself that no matter how strong an image he projected, it would take time to attract a following. He brushed his disappointment aside and went to work on the next client's project. The old movie line had another consequence—he'd been inspired to watch a film that evening, and take a break from his networking and client work.

Building a great LinkedIn profile page is a start, but it's only the first step.

Photographer Dave was friendly and efficient at the afternoon shoot, and Gnik returned home to download his photos from a flash drive. He quickly selected a favorite head-shot and posted it to his LinkedIn profile. Satisfied with the results, he searched his DVD collection for a movie to match his mood.

As he flipped though the discs, he recalled Pam saying his laptop could be a computer or a miniature movie theater. "That's what my laptop is tonight," he said aloud to the empty apartment as his eyes fell on the *The Wizard of Oz.* He removed the disc and slid it into the drive on his laptop. He put his headphones over his ears, adjusted the screen, and lost himself in the movie. The DVD had been the gift of a friend several years earlier, and he returned to the movie now and again, always learning something new or reinforcing a lesson learned previously.

As he immersed himself in the action, something caught his attention in a way he had never noticed before. He replayed the scene.

Dorothy asked, "But how do I start?"

"It's always best to start at the beginning," Glinda the Good Witch said. "Just follow the Yellow Brick Road."

Glinda's advice resounded in Gnik's head, but he didn't quite know why.

Just follow the yellow brick road?

Another replay of Glinda's counsel seemed to answer his question. *It's always best to start at the beginning.* He paused the movie and thought about Garrett's question again.

How am I going to use LinkedIn? Maybe I should start at the beginning. Wherever that is.

Pausing the movie and minimizing the window, Gnik opened a browser tab. Why not start at the beginning *with a coach who can help expedite the process*? He typed into the search window:

Learn LinkedIn Fast

Of the search results that displayed instantly on his screen, one item caught his attention. It seemed to say to him, "Gnik Rowten, meet Victoria Ipri!"

Gnik's Aha!

To be successful on LinkedIn I must be focused and purposeful. I need to know what it is I want to accomplish.

day 4

Get Clear on Your Goals

The alarm on Gnik's nightstand rang for a few seconds before he realized that morning had arrived. He swung out of bed and rubbed his eyes, as if pushing away the darkness to allow dawn to enter. Now able to focus on the tasks that awaited him, he completed his morning ritual and emerged from his bedroom ready to seize the day.

Picking up his tablet, he scanned the website he had bookmarked the previous night. He found encouragement in a quote from Victoria Ipri.

**You don't need to know *everything* about LinkedIn.
You only need to know what you need to know.
And then you need to put it into action.**

The advice eased his mind. *Putting it into action? I can do that. So it's really just a matter of knowing what I need to know.*

The website described a webinar that Gnik thought might help him clarify his LinkedIn goals. He signed up for the next session and made a note on his calendar. Then he reviewed his schedule for the day and gathered all the resources he'd need for his client meetings and projects. He walked out of his apartment and headed to his first appointment.

Gnik had been working with Mark, the owner of a home healthcare business, for several months and was ready to present some new ideas for his marketing campaign. They sat in Mark's office and chatted about news, sports, and the weather before getting down to business; when the subject turned to the social networks, Gnik reminded Mark that they were connected on LinkedIn.

"That's true," Mark nodded.

"I'm trying to be a bit more proactive in connecting with people," Gnik said, warming to the subject. "I've done a pretty good job at face-to-face networking, but I think there's value in taking more of it online."

"It certainly lets you overcome geographical limitations," Mark said. "I've been able to meet people around the country, even around the world."

So far, Gnik had reached out to friends and colleagues on LinkedIn but hadn't used it to meet new people, as Mark was doing. "Tell me more," he said.

"When I started using LinkedIn, I just connected with people I already knew," Mark said. "In fact, at first I was afraid to reach out to anyone I didn't know because I didn't want to be 'penalized' for trying to connect with people who didn't know me. I took a pretty conservative approach."

"Sounds like me," Gnik nodded. "What changed?"

Mark continued. "I had joined a LinkedIn group for home healthcare administrators and was learning a lot about best practices. One day I received a connection request from another member of the group. I had seen her comments on various issues, and she'd apparently seen some of mine, too, and liked them. The whole thing seemed so natural ... I never really thought about the fact that we didn't know each other until after I'd accepted her invitation to connect."

Gnik liked what he was hearing. "So you're in favor of connecting with people you don't really know?"

"Absolutely. The way my LinkedIn network has grown, it's mostly people I share common interests with but haven't met in person. I've developed some great business and personal relationships that way, even if most of them are only virtual."

After concluding his business with Mark, Gnik headed to the coffee shop. Victoria Ipri's LinkedIn webinar would be starting soon, so he turned on his laptop, navigated to her website, put on his headphones, and prepared to absorb whatever she was ready to share.

The webcast started and Victoria introduced herself to her unseen group of attendees.

"You may feel like LinkedIn is a foreign language," she said. "And it is! Fortunately, I'm fluent in the language of LinkedIn." She quoted the line from her website that had gotten Gnik's attention that morning: "You don't need to know *everything* about LinkedIn ..."

From his seat in the coffee shop, Gnik gave her comment a thumbs-up.

"First, let's talk semantics," Victoria continued. "On LinkedIn, a 'contact' is someone saved to your contacts list because either you've sent an invitation to connect that they have not yet accepted, or you've sent them a message through the LinkedIn platform. People can be saved as a contact when you sync them from other sources, like your Gmail address book, or you've saved their profile after viewing it ..."

Gnik made a mental note. *Contacts are people you've already "messaged" or invited to connect on LinkedIn.*

"... but they're not a 'connection' until you accept their request to connect or they accept yours. When that happens, they become a First Degree connection. LinkedIn has *connections*—not friends. If you're on Facebook, you have friends."

Gnik chuckled at the notion that a Facebook connection magically conferred friendship, and made another mental note to the effect that *"Connections" on LinkedIn are like "friends" on Facebook.*

"The connections of LinkedIn members you know and are connected with have their own connections—they are your Second Degree network. *Their* connections are your Third Degree. Together, all three levels comprise your LinkedIn network, which will also include the people you follow in your groups."

"Interesting," Gnik whispered, aware that he was in a public place.

Next Victoria talked about how people use the network. "People may think that if you build your profile, 'they will come,'" she said, and Gnik remembered thinking precisely that just yesterday. "Or, they don't realize that LinkedIn is far more than a site to look for jobs. It's a place to build a business."

This insight hit Gnik in a new way. Mark had helped him recognize the power of connecting to people you don't know, but he hadn't considered the concept of actually building a business using LinkedIn. He listened intently as Victoria spoke briefly about the concept of company pages for those running businesses, before wrapping up her presentation.

"Start looking for people," she concluded. "Look for coworkers, peers, and colleagues. Think about your reason for connecting with them. What is your goal for the relationship?"

The webinar ended and Gnik brought his attention back to Garrett's question, "How are you going to use LinkedIn?" Opening his notebook, he wrote three answers.

1. Connect with people who share my interests

2. Expand my network beyond my existing circle of friends

3. Build my business

Gnik wasn't sure exactly how he would attack the latter two, but he was excited about the possibilities with LinkedIn. From Victoria's webpage he clicked the "Talk to Victoria" link and typed a short message.

> Victoria, I was on your webinar today and want to thank you for your time and insight. I have a much better understanding of what LinkedIn is, and how I can use it in my own network and business.
>
> You have helped me understand the language of LinkedIn.
>
> Thank you.
> Gnik (With a "G")

He pressed the Send button and set his notes aside. He left the coffee shop for additional appointments and returned to his apartment late in the day. Eager to continue his LinkedIn education, he settled into his thinking chair and opened his laptop.

Gnik's Aha!

I don't need to know *everything* about LinkedIn. I only need to know what I need to know. Then, I need to put it into action.

day 5

Create a Winning Profile

The morning was cold and overcast. Gnik pushed the curtains aside, cracked open the window, and smiled. In spite of the weather, he knew it was going to be a great day.

Resisting the urge to hole up in his apartment and get lost in email and blog posts, he prepared for his day's work and headed to his favorite coffee shop. He hadn't planned to meet with Pam, but subconsciously hoped he'd bump into her while enjoying his morning java. There was a smattering of customers in the place, but his regular table was empty. He arranged his computer and notepad in a tight radius, leaving room for another patron to sit down.

He turned on his laptop and leaned back as the system started up, then opened his email. Skimming the incoming messages, he saw a LinkedIn notification from Whitney. His stomach tightened.

She invited me to connect with her ... why am I nervous? He clicked on the message and saw that Whitney indeed had accepted his connection request. She'd also included a reply with a lively message.

> There once was a fellow named Gnik.
> We met on an airplane and clicked.
> His speeches are boring.
> The audience is snoring.
> His marketing better be slick!
>
> Gnik, I'd love to learn a little about how I can improve my marketing, and I'm happy to help you with your presentations. A quick FYI, though. Whenever people reach out to me on LinkedIn, I always look at their profile to see who I'm connecting with.
>
> To be frank, your profile seemed a little dull. As I read it againaaalfaaaaaaaaaaaaaaaaaaa . . .
>
> Sorry, I nodded off. You may want to take another look at that baby and spice it up a bit.
>
> Let's talk soon, and I'm sorry if my sense of humor is a little over the top today.
>
> Glad we've connected on LinkedIn!
>
> Whitney

Gnik's face grew red with embarrassment. He looked around instinctively, feeling as if all eyes must be on him, but no one seemed to notice. He read the message again, hoping it was somehow more flattering than it seemed the first time.

It wasn't. He opened his profile page to see if he could recognize what Whitney saw. He recalled the pleasure he'd felt the other day when he finished filling in the blanks and thought it was mission accomplished. LinkedIn had even upgraded his profile to "Expert."

One look and he knew she was right. This might be "Expert," but experts can be boring. *Would I want to connect with someone who comes off this bland?* He was going to have to rework the profile again, but although he considered himself a skilled writer he really didn't know where to start. *If I'm going to have a winning day today, I'd better figure out how to produce a winning profile.*

He opened a new tab on his browser and searched "LinkedIn profile makeover." Clicking on a few top links, he realized that a number of them were pointing to the same name: Donna Serdula.

Gnik dialed the phone number on Donna's website, and as he heard the ringing through his earpiece he suddenly questioned what he was doing. *This is going right to voicemail, anyway,* he figured, relaxing. *I'll leave a message and that'll be that.*

On the third ring, however, a soft voice answered.

"Donna Serdula. How can I help you?"

Gnik nearly stumbled on his first words, but quickly regained his composure. "Hi, Donna. I didn't actually think you'd pick up."

She laughed. "I get that a lot. Are you calling about my profile makeovers?"

"I am. A friend told me in a not-so-gentle way that my LinkedIn profile could use some help. I had no idea where to start, so I did a search and your name came up."

Donna's bright, friendly tone put Gnik immediately at ease. "I've worked with thousands of individuals to help them improve their profiles. Tell me a little about yourself and what you do."

Gnik gave an abbreviated version of his story, from the time he left his position with a marketing firm, to moving to a new city and starting his own business. He finished with a question.

"Why do I need an elaborate LinkedIn profile, Donna? I've added most of the details LinkedIn suggests, but my friend finds it boring with a capital 'B.' I know it's not exactly a thrilling read, but I'm not sure why it needs to be."

She answered enthusiastically. "I love that question, Gnik. Let me answer by asking you, would you go to a business conference wearing cutoff jeans and a stained T-shirt?"

"Of course not."

"Exactly. Your LinkedIn profile is your business suit. It shows people your value, your attitude, and who you are. It should compel them to reach out to you, and more importantly, to feel good about you. In your case, Gnik, if you can't market *yourself*, who's going to trust you to market their business?"

"I never thought about it that way. So what's the secret of a winning profile?"

"There's a lot that you *can* do, but there are some basics. First, you need a picture—a professionally taken headshot, not a selfie. Remember, this is your brand you're establishing and you want the world to see you in the best possible light."

Your LinkedIn profile should be more than a compilation of details. To attract people, it must showcase your individuality.

"Makes sense," Gnik agreed. "I've already done that."

"Excellent. Next, you need a strong headline. It's not enough just to list your job titles and company. You need a benefit statement that is infused with keywords. You want people to feel compelled to learn more about you when they read it. Don't give them an excuse to move on to the next profile."

"It sounds like it should be more of a narrative than a list," Gnik said.

"Exactly!" Donna's enthusiasm was obvious. "And your *summary* should also be a narrative. Write it in First Person and make it conversational. What does your target market need to hear from you? Tell them who you are and what you offer. Don't leave them with bullet points. Make it *personal.* People will be more likely to connect with you if they feel they know you, and a well-written profile will let them glimpse into the window of your brand. They'll feel comfortable with you, and may be more willing to connect. You can even include a call to action: Invite people to contact you."

"Wow—I can see how that could make a difference." Gnik felt renewed enthusiasm, as the target he wanted his profile to hit came into sharper focus.

"It will," Donna promised. "If you're using LinkedIn to connect with potential clients or customers, you want to make it easy for them to connect with you. Your profile should make it easy for them to see what you're all about. Your profile sells *you.* It's not your resume. It needs to pop!

"Use *keywords*—the words people will type into a search engine when they're looking for someone like you," she continued. "Include them in your headline, summary, and past experiences. Also, include relevant skills ... order them so that the most important ones are at the top. Write your profile as if you were having a conversation with someone. It's not a list of accomplishments, it's your career future!

To be effective, a LinkedIn profile requires a personal touch that casts you and your business in a distinctive light. People respond to personalities rather than to lists of degrees and achievements.

Donna described some of the profile resources available on her website and offered to help Gnik create a winning profile. "You may want to set up a vanity URL," she added.

"Come again?" Gnik said.

She explained. "When you set up your account, the link to your profile will appear as randomly generated letters and numbers. When you edit your profile, find the option to customize the URL and change it to something memorable, like your name."

After thanking Donna for her time, Gnik dedicated the rest of the afternoon to enhancing his profile. As the sky began to darken outside the coffee shop, he gathered his belongings and returned home.

Pleased with the day's accomplishments, Gnik settled into his chair, opened his laptop, and clicked to view his freshly updated profile again.

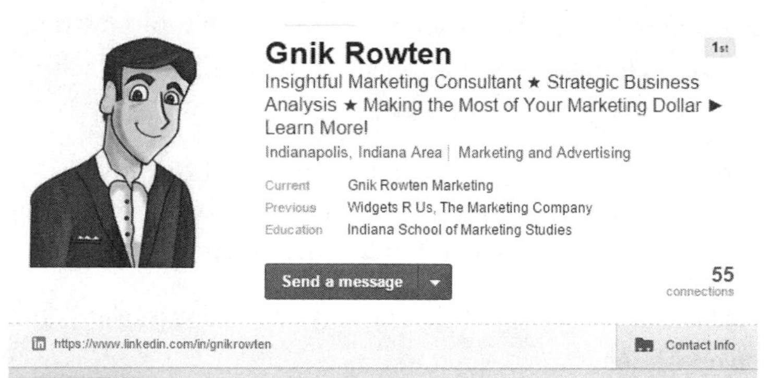

Background

 Summary

★ Do you need help getting your product or service to stand out in a crowded market?

★ Would you like to get your brand in front of the right eyes to make the most of your marketing budget?

My name is Gnik Rowten, and as an experienced Marketing & Communications professional, I bring fresh perspectives and deep insight into current and future marketing trends.

With a passion for connecting people, I help companies create successful and profitable business relationships and expand their circle of influence.

I'm on LinkedIn to build and nurture strong, strategic relationships.

Let's connect ► gnik@gnikrowten.com

 Experience

Marketing Consultant ► Helping Businesses Take Their Marketing to the Next Level
Gnik Rowten Marketing
2014 – Present (1 year) | Indianapolis, Indiana Area

Gnik Rowten Marketing was established in 2014 to help area businesses develop fresh perspectives and deep insights into current and future marketing trends.

He smiled with satisfaction at the improvement and returned to Whitney's email from that morning. Reading it now with a different mindset, he typed a reply.

> Whitney, thank you for being honest about my profile—you helped me realize how much better it could be. I'm looking forward to talking again.

Content, he powered off his laptop and went into the kitchen to make dinner.

Gnik's Aha!

My LinkedIn profile is like my business suit. It needs to show the world my values, my attitude, and who I am.

day 6

Develop Your Connection Strategy

Bundled up under a thick comforter, Gnik felt protected from the morning chill in his apartment. But the momentum of the past few days had energized him and he had no reluctance to leave his bed's warm embrace.

As he showered and dressed, Gnik reviewed the insights he had gained from Victoria's webinar two days earlier. *I can use LinkedIn to build my business.* The prospect energized him, as he sat down to devise a plan for establishing his brand. Between spoonfuls of granola, he jotted down three concepts that had been swirling in his head.

1. Proactively connect with the people I already know.
2. Proactively seek out and connect with people I want to add to my network.

3. Learn how to use LinkedIn to generate business.

He paused, realizing that there was an aspect of his connection strategy he had been overlooking. *What about the people who reach out to* me*? Is there reason to be cautious about whose invitations I accept?*

Gnik hadn't yet faced that dilemma; so far, only people whom he knew had reached out to him on LinkedIn, but he realized that would change as his exposure increased. He added a fourth item to his to-do list, and then a fifth, based on something Victoria had said.

4. Clarify strategy for incoming connection requests.

5. Think about creating a company page.

He felt satisfied as he cleared the breakfast dishes from his kitchen table; the simple act seemed to represent removing the clutter from his approach to LinkedIn. He sat down at the table with his notepad and pen in front of him; even in the digital age, writing in longhand was oddly satisfying for Gnik. It seemed to help him better focus his thoughts.

He underlined each of his five to-do's and began to flesh them out.

1. *Proactively connect with the people I already know.*

It should be pretty easy to connect on LinkedIn with people I know from school and work, and other friends and acquaintances. Just do it.

Gnik recalled LinkedIn's option that would enable him to import email addresses of people he knew. *That simplifies matters—that's how I'll connect with them.*

He began to expand on the second item on his list.

2. *Proactively seek out and connect with people I want to add to my network.*

This is about more than just compiling a list of names. I need to find and connect with people I have something important in common with. If they're in the marketing business we could connect to share ideas, but that's just one type of connection. I need to give this a lot more thought.

3. *Learn how to use LinkedIn to generate business.*

Gnik tapped his pen on the table nervously. *I don't even know where to start on this one.* He put a star next to the number 3 and made a mental note to pursue this goal as he got more comfortable and confident using LinkedIn. He moved on to the next part of his plan.

4. *Clarify strategy for incoming connection requests.*

He sat back in his chair and clasped his hands behind his head. He felt he didn't know enough about the benefits or risks of connecting with unknown people to be able to make an informed decision now.

"I wonder what Pam would say," he said to himself. He'd met Pam when he first moved to the city, and she had since become a friend and mentor whose perspective he deeply valued.

Gnik's call to Pam went right to voicemail, so he moved on to the last point on his list.

5. *Think about creating a company page.*

Victoria had spoken briefly about company pages, so Gnik turned to his notes from the webinar to refresh his memory. *My current LinkedIn page is my personal presence that allows people to view my profile, grasp what I'm about, and connect with me if they want to. A company page, on the other hand, would give people an opportunity to learn specifically about my business.* The concept made complete sense to him.

The phone's ring interrupted his thoughts. Pam's name was on the Caller ID and he quickly answered.

"How are you, Pam?"

"Good to hear from you, Gnik. What's up?"

He explained his concern. "I'm working on my connection strategy for LinkedIn, and trying to decide how to handle it when people I've never heard of invite me to connect. What types of things should I consider before making a decision?"

"Excellent question, Gnik. There are basically two schools of thought and even experts can't agree. You may decide you only want people in your network who you know personally. People you would be comfortable vouching for, for instance, if the situation arose."

"Okay ..."

"On the other hand, if you refuse to connect with anyone and *everyone* you don't know personally, you're likely to miss out on some potentially useful, even important connections. You're going to have to make that decision for yourself, possibly on a case-by-case basis. What is it you want to accomplish?"

Gnik thought about that for a moment. "Suppose I'm willing to connect with anyone—what are the risks?"

Pam chuckled. "Risks? I can't name all the risks, because new ones always come up. But there are some things to be aware of. When you connect with someone, you're granting access to everything you post on your profile page. If you connect with a spammer, you open yourself up to receiving junk messages or possibly even having spam sent in your name. If you connect with a direct competitor, and you allow your connections to see one other, your competition will be able to see who's in your network. I don't have to spell it out for you, I guess."

"I hadn't even thought about competitive risks. Yikes."

"It really comes down to deciding how *open* you want to be. Me? I'm pretty open, but I like to know why someone wants to connect with me. If I don't see any shared interest, and the person isn't connected to others in my network, I'll usually click the little 'x' and ignore the invitation."

Don't automatically comply with an unknown person's request to connect.

"That makes sense," Gnik said. "You've given me plenty to think about." He thanked Pam for her time and insight, and returned to his strategy document. As to his question, he decided to remain open to connecting but cautious about who to let through the gate. As Pam had suggested, he'd want to consider *why* someone might want to connect with him before accepting an invitation.

Satisfied by how quickly his strategy framework was coming together, Gnik put his notebook aside, checked his watch, and realized he had just enough time to get to his noon meeting.

Gnik's Aha!

It's important to develop a rationale for how I connect on LinkedIn.

day 7

Make Time to Grow Your Network

Gnik woke early enough to walk out his door just as the sun was creeping over the horizon. The cool air felt good, and as he took a deep breath, he felt mentally sharp in advance of the breakfast networking event he'd decided to attend.

When he'd first moved to the city, Gnik had gone to several such events, and they'd helped him build a strong and still growing group of friends and business contacts. Though recently he'd been focused on increasing his LinkedIn presence, he never discounted the value and enjoyment of face-to-face interaction. *I've missed these live networking events,* he was thinking as his feet hit the sidewalk.

He walked through the city's downtown maze until arriving at the event location. Reaching into his pocket, he felt his business card holder and smiled as he thought back to one meeting where a man in a purple shirt had passed out business cards like a blackjack dealer. The man's rapid-fire, "all about me" system had not impressed Gnik, who managed to avoid Purple Shirt while watching, amused, as he corralled one unsuspecting victim after another.

Looking around the room, he decided to approach a man and woman who appeared engaged in casual conversation. Seeing Gnik, the man spoke first. "Come join us. I'm Matt Scherer and this is my new friend, Allison." Gnik introduced himself and the three shook hands.

"Matt and I were talking about how the art of in-person networking seems to be less of a priority for many people as they take their networking online," Allison said. She nudged Matt playfully and continued. "I'm a proponent of face-to-face networking, but Matt's been trying to convince me to do more on LinkedIn. What about you?"

Sensing the light mood, Gnik employed a mock serious tone. "I just got here, Allison. It's too early for me to make any enemies." The three of them laughed together. *Whitney would be proud of me,* Gnik thought.

Matt got the conversation back on track. "I'm curious about your thoughts, Gnik. You're here, so I'm guessing you find in-person networking useful. What's your take on using LinkedIn and other social sites as part of a networking strategy?"

"When I first moved here, I was all about these kinds of meetings—shaking hands, exchanging cards, following up on the phone," Gnik recalled. "I learned a great deal about building connections in person, but I was really neglecting the online side. I kind of assumed that networking was networking, with no real advantage to connecting online versus meeting face-to-face."

Matt and Allison nodded, cueing him to continue.

"But it's funny you should ask, Matt, because about a week ago I started focusing on my online networking—specifically to strengthen my LinkedIn network. I have my work cut out for me."

"I do a lot on LinkedIn," Matt said. "I really like meeting people in person, but I think professionals need to be just as smart building their LinkedIn networks as they are about the offline stuff."

Allison interjected with the same thought that had popped into Gnik's head. "What do you mean by *smart*?"

Matt pointed across the room. "See that woman in the navy pantsuit? She approached me when I first arrived and asked if I needed my home refinanced. I told her no and she asked if I knew anyone who did. She shoved her business card into my hand and asked me to give her a call if I came up with any leads. She actually used that word. *Leads!*"

Gnik thought about the guy in the purple shirt again. "Are you saying people do that on LinkedIn, too?"

Matt nodded. "Absolutely. I get connection requests all the time from people I don't know. I don't mind that, necessarily. What I *do* mind are the people who have no interest in me or anything I do. They just see that I have a lot of connections and want to use me to grow their network."

"So you're saying you'll only connect online with people you've met in person?" Allison asked.

"Not at all. But I do expect them to have a reason to connect with me beyond access to my network. Maybe they've read my blog and liked what I said. Maybe they want to leverage LinkedIn to grow their business, which is what I write about. Maybe they're military—see, I also have a military background. That's the type of thing I'm looking for: a reason to connect in the first place."

Online or off, networking is about more than making a high volume of contacts.

"That makes sense," said Gnik. "You're trying to separate the wheat from the chaff."

"Exactly," Matt said. "Take the three of us—we've spent a few minutes together and, frankly, I've enjoyed our conversation. I'd love to continue it online." He turned to Allison. "Think you're ready to take the LinkedIn plunge?"

"I've been successfully resisting it so far," Allison grinned.

"I haven't been so successful, Matt," Gnik admitted. "Let's connect."

"Great!" Matt handed Gnik and Allison each a business card. Gnik looked at the card, which included the URL for Matt's blog. "You can connect with me here," Matt said, pointing to the information. "I make it easy."

Gnik agreed and looked at his own card. It had a reference to LinkedIn, but didn't make connecting as clear-cut as Matt's did.

Matt continued his connection tutorial. "When you connect with me, remind me of this conversation. And when you're looking to connect with others, ask to connect with them on LinkedIn *after* you've already established some sort of conversation. Don't start with the connection request. Otherwise, you're like the pantsuit lady."

"Before breakfast starts, Matt, what's your thinking on connecting with people you don't know?" Gnik asked.

"It's the same principle. Have a reason to connect. Don't send out random connection requests and hope that something sticks—that's what a telemarketer does. Be sure you have something in common."

Make a personal conversation a prerequisite to connecting with someone on LinkedIn.

"You'll need to be proactive," Matt continued. "Schedule time regularly to find people you want to connect with. Take the lead. Say something like, 'I like your perspective on such and such,' or 'I'm working for a client and looking for someone who has your expertise.' Be patient. Not everyone is looking at LinkedIn every day."

"And you find that works?"

Matt nodded. "Tell me how you would respond to someone telling you, 'I like what you have to say about crafting a marketing message and would like to speak with you at some point.' Would you connect with them?"

"I would."

"You bet you would ... So, Gnik, what do you say we get together for a virtual cup of coffee sometime?"

"Love to."

"You, too, Allison?" Matt said.

"Sure, I'm game," she said. "First I'm going to have to revisit LinkedIn and figure out what the heck it's all about."

Later, during the breakfast, Gnik glanced at Matt's card again. He would be sure to reach out to this guy on LinkedIn. Opening his calendar, he scheduled an hour the next morning to work on his connections.

Gnik's Aha!

It makes sense to connect with people with whom I have an overlapping purpose or shared interest.

day 8

Understand the Power of Groups

Gnik started his day with a plan to expand his LinkedIn network. *I need to schedule regular time for connection-building on LinkedIn and stick to my schedule.* A consistent approach was key, he felt certain.

Looking at his calendar, he realized that today was Garrett's birthday. He pulled up Garrett's LinkedIn profile and sent a message:

> Happy birthday, Garrett! Thanks for being part of my LinkedIn network. Hope it's a great day for you.

While browsing Garrett's profile, Gnik's cursor hovered over "Connections" on the top menu bar. An option he hadn't noticed before emerged: Keep in Touch. Curious, he clicked the link, and a list of profile pictures popped up, with new job and work anniversary details listed. He took a few minutes to send congratulatory messages to a couple of his connections who had new jobs and anniversaries. Then he gave some thought to whom he might invite to connect on LinkedIn.

Matt Scherer from yesterday was first up. He placed the man's business card on his desk and typed the URL, which instantly brought up Matt's website. Gnik clicked the "Contact" link and typed a message:

> Matt, I enjoyed our conversation about LinkedIn yesterday and was particularly intrigued by your thoughts on making connections. I'd love to continue the conversation.

After sending the message he decided to connect with some of the other people he'd interacted with during the past week, including Victoria Ipri and Donna Serdula. After sending connection requests to them, he noticed that he'd already received a response from Garrett.

> Gnik, it's good to hear from you. Thank you for the kind wishes. I want to introduce you to a friend who may be able to help you as you learn the power of LinkedIn. I met Jason Alba through one of the LinkedIn groups I belong to, and he's got a unique perspective that you'll be interested in. I've told him to expect your call.

Garrett's note concluded with Jason's contact information and the suggestion that he try calling him first. Gnik looked at his watch and saw that he'd been working on networking activities for 15 minutes. *I can commit at least a few minutes a day to building my network.* He didn't want to waste time on the networking site and knew how easily he could get distracted if he wasn't careful. *I have plenty to do today without getting sidetracked.* He closed his laptop and prepared for the meetings and projects he'd scheduled for the day.

I can always find at least a few minutes a day to devote to building my network.

By the early afternoon Gnik had made good progress and found himself with some free time. He picked up the phone and dialed the number Garrett had provided earlier. Jason answered on the first ring.

"Hi, Jason—it's Gnik Rowten, Garrett's friend. He suggested I speak with you about LinkedIn. Do you have any time to talk now?"

"I sure do," Jason said. "I'm always happy to talk about LinkedIn."

"Great. So how do you know Garrett?"

"We met on LinkedIn," Jason said. "In fact, he was in one of the first groups I joined."

"He probably told you I'm new to LinkedIn groups, but I'm interested ... what do I need to know?"

Jason explained that groups within LinkedIn are communities of people with something in common, such as a particular industry or other professional interest. "Joining the right groups is one of the best ways to proactively network on LinkedIn, I think," he said.

"So how does it work?" Gnik was intrigued.

"When you network, you want to associate with people who are relevant to you, right? Well, if you join the right group—*right* because it deals with your profession, your industry, or even your geography—you have the best chance of making productive connections."

"I follow you," Gnik said. "It's all about sharing common interests."

"Precisely. So, go to the Groups page on LinkedIn and see what jumps out at you. Look for groups that fit one, two, or even three of the criteria I mentioned—same profession, industry, or geography. Groups like that are bound to have members who are relevant to you in some way. Also look at the size of the group. Some have a few members; others have thousands. If you join a large group, you make it easy for thousands of people to communicate with you, instantly."

"I hadn't even considered that." Gnik was starting to understand the possibilities.

Joining the right groups gives you the opportunity to interact with the widest circle of likeminded people on LinkedIn.

"Broadly speaking, there are a couple of advantages to joining a group," Jason said. "You expand both your reach and your *reachability*."

"That makes sense," Gnik said.

"Of course, just joining a group doesn't mean that someone you want to have a conversation with will instantly reach out to you. The power, however, is in your ability to reach out to members of the group. So choose your groups wisely. If there's someone you want to find, and you can identify a group that he or she is in, joining that group will give you an opportunity to engage in a dialog."

"There must be a lot of groups to choose from."

Jason laughed. "There are indeed. Do some research. See what people are writing. Look for relevant discussions and comment on them. That's how you join the conversation. When you comment, you start to show up consistently in the inboxes of contributors and others who receive notifications of updates to the conversations. Eventually, you can become quite well known within the group community."

"I like it," Gnik said. "And I can see how becoming active in a group might help me to develop my personal brand."

"Now you're with the program!" Jason said approvingly. "Oh, and if you don't want daily notification emails from every group you join, turn off the notifications. You can still manually check on a group's activity anytime you like."

Gnik thanked Jason and wrapped up the conversation by asking if he could add him to his LinkedIn network, which he did immediately after hanging up.

This changes how I'll use LinkedIn. Gnik let the possibilities swim through his mind. *I can't wait to check out some groups*!

Gnik's Aha!

Joining relevant groups will accelerate my ability to add people with common interests to my network.

day 9

Take the Leap Into Groups

Joining the right groups is one of the best ways to proactively network on LinkedIn, Gnik remembered Jason telling him the day before. He opened his LinkedIn profile page and found "Groups" listed under "Interests." Clicking the "Find a group" link, he decided to enter the name of his alma mater for starters.

Several groups instantly popped up that, judging from the numbers of members and "discussions," appeared to be quite well established. There were many others with fewer participants, as well, and he realized he wouldn't have any trouble at all finding one or more groups to join. His first thought was to be selective, at least to start, rather than joining them all.

As he spent some time reading the profiles of various groups associated with his college, Gnik discovered that some were private, requiring that his membership be approved. He clicked on the *Join* button for one that particularly intrigued him, discovering a link for adjusting group settings near the top of the page.

Not yet an official member of the group, he followed the link and quickly understood what Jason had meant about turning off notifications: He could receive an email message each time a new discussion was started, or receive a single daily or weekly "digest" email covering all of the group's activity. He decided that, for the college group, he wanted to be informed but didn't need to be notified about *every* new discussion. So he kept the default setting to receive a weekly digest, and also left the box checked that permitted group members to send him messages.

Next, Gnik searched groups associated with his former company, the city where he lived, and the city where he'd grown up. He found groups that focused on his hobbies, his marketing interests, and even a couple that discussed areas he wanted to grow into in his business. He checked the settings for each group he requested to join, just to be sure he wouldn't be overwhelmed with group-related email. By the end of his searching session, Gnik had joined three groups that did not require approval and applied to 19 that did. His membership in those 19 groups was shown as "pending."

To be successful, Gnik reflected, a networker has to be visible. *People can't connect with me if they don't know I exist.* Applying this wisdom—gained from his in-person networking experience—to his new online memberships, he sensed that his involvement in group discussions would be the best way for other members to get to know him. *I don't want to start a new discussion yet,* he decided. *I don't know enough yet about group content or dynamics. But I* am *curious about what's happening in the existing discussions.* He scrolled through some of the discussions hosted by the open groups he had just joined and picked a couple that caught his interest.

As he read the comments on one of the discussion threads, he noticed that one participant in particular had something relevant to add in almost every case. Her name was Katelyn, and she came across as a leader in some of the discussions, but when he checked he saw that she was neither the group owner nor one of its managers. *I guess Jason was right when he said that getting involved will put my name out there. Katelyn certainly has done that.*

If they're to connect with me, people need to know I exist. But that's not enough. For my connections to be powerful, I must have the confidence to share my perspective in group forums.

Given the number of groups he'd applied to, Gnik reviewed the list and decided there were a few that he could do without. *If I'm going to use my group memberships to enhance my personal branding strategy, I should make sure that my groups are relevant to my interests and goals—both business and personal.* He withdrew his membership in those groups, then returned to one of the open groups and found a discussion that appealed to him. After reading the thread, he added a fresh thought to the discussion. He entered some other discussions, then went back to Katelyn. *I feel like I know her just from reading her comments.* Recalling Matt's emphasis on taking the lead in developing connections, he decided to reach out to Katelyn.

Gnik clicked on her profile and immediately noted their shared interests. LinkedIn made it easy for him to connect with Katelyn through a group, even though she was not yet part of his network. He wanted to change that in a hurry and clicked the "Connect" button on her profile to customize his connection request:

> Katelyn, I've been reading your comments on City's Marketing Network group posts, and I like your perspective. I'd love to share some marketing ideas directly.

He sent the request, returned to the group, clicked on the Members tab, and browsed other group members, noticing that several were Second Degree connections for him. Because they shared group membership, Gnik could send connection requests to these members, inviting them to become First Degree connections.

He opened his email program and saw that a couple of his chosen groups had already approved his membership. "This has been a good day," he said to himself.

Gnik's Aha!

Groups give me access to people and give people access to me—even if we're not directly connected.

day 10

The Road to Credibility

Morning came, and Gnik arose thinking about the many groups he'd applied to the previous day. He opened his email and was pleased to see that his membership had already been approved for most of them. Another message caught his attention as well:

> Andy, Cindy, and Beth have endorsed you!
>
> Congratulations, Gnik! You have been endorsed for the following skills: Vendor Management, Software Documentation, and Customer Satisfaction.

Gnik rolled his eyes, thinking, *Sure, I've got some experience with vendor management and customer satisfaction, but I've never done anything with software documentation. Where did* that *come from?*

He opened his LinkedIn profile and navigated to the Skills and Endorsements section, where he saw a small but growing list of skills that other people had attributed to him. With a little effort he found the place in the settings where he could opt out of being endorsed, but decided he'd wait to learn more about the function first. A local presentation featuring JD Gershbein speaking about recommendations on LinkedIn was scheduled to start in an hour, and he thought he might get some answers there.

Arriving at the conference center early, Gnik took a seat near the front of the auditorium. A professional-looking woman took a seat next to him, and Gnik didn't hesitate.

"Hi. I'm Gnik. That's with a 'G.'"

"Hi, Gnik, I'm Aubrie. With an 'A.' Tell me about your name."

Once again, my name comes in handy as a conversation starter. Gnik smiled. "Sure, Aubrie," he said. "My full name, Gnik Rowten, is 'networking' spelled backward. Can you believe my parents' creativity?"

Aubrie chuckled. "Love it. And it certainly is memorable. I guess you must be a natural at networking, then."

"Not really, but I'm learning."

"So what brings you here? Do you know JD?"

"I don't, but I've been trying to do more with LinkedIn. I haven't done much with recommendations or endorsements yet, so I'm looking forward to what he has to say."

They exchanged business cards and Gnik reached for his notepad as JD walked onstage. The presentation was especially timely for Gnik, considering the email he'd received this morning. One of the first things JD mentioned was that there is generally no rhyme or reason for endorsements.

"Endorsements on LinkedIn are merely superficial acknowledgments of a skill," he said. "Users endorse each other because they are being prompted to do so. *Recommendations*, on the other hand, are pure engagement, requiring one-on-one interaction.

"When I get an endorsement from someone I truly respect, however, for a skill I actually *have*, I like to go back to them and thank them. Many times the dialog continues offline."

Gnik looked up from his note-taking as if he'd had a revelation.

LinkedIn facilitates communication, but it's up to the user to take the initiative and engage others in conversation.

"Written recommendations are far more meaningful assessments of skills and expertise than endorsements," JD continued. "They are much more effective in establishing your credibility. In fact, a written recommendation is the only source of user-generated content that will show up on your profile."

At the close of the presentation, Gnik joined a number of other attendees who wanted to meet and thank the speaker.

"Your presentation was very timely for me," Gnik said. "This morning I received an endorsement for a skill I don't have."

JD advised Gnik to modify his endorsements so that the skills he wanted highlighted came first, and irrelevant skills were eliminated. "If you don't have a skill, or you're being endorsed by people who don't know you well enough to know whether you have it, it's okay to sort the endorsements—or delete them—to reflect the branding you want."

Gnik nodded. "I'll take care of that when I get home."

Turning to leave, JD said, "Never take any positive action—no matter how small—for granted. Express gratitude and continue the conversation. People will tend to reciprocate."

Gnik thanked him for his time and asked if they could connect on LinkedIn. JD said he'd be happy to, and they exchanged cards.

After leaving the conference center, Gnik called a couple of clients to update them on the marketing proposals he was preparing for them. Next stop: the coffee shop. He sat in his regular seat and stretched his legs under the table. He powered on his tablet, brought up his LinkedIn profile, and reviewed his Skills and Endorsements section. He was still getting used to navigating LinkedIn on his smaller screen, but with a little effort he was able to rearrange his skills so they made sense and delete a couple that didn't apply.

Next, because he wanted to be in a position to continue the conversation with any connection who endorsed him, Gnik opted to receive emails notifying him of new endorsements. He saved his settings before spending a few minutes endorsing his contacts for what he considered their notable skills. He sent thank you messages to Andy, Cindy, and Beth, who had all endorsed him.

It's been a long but productive day, and I haven't even gotten to JD's suggestions on recommendations, he thought as he turned his tablet off. *I'll prioritize that tomorrow.*

Collecting his things and placing them in his backpack, Gnik waved to the barista as he left the coffee shop. "See you tomorrow."

Gnik's Aha!

I want to make sure that LinkedIn endorsements on my behalf are consistent with my skills and expertise, and organized to my best advantage.

day 11

Ye Shall Give and Receive Recommendations

Gnik woke up thinking about the value of written recommendations and how to add them to his profile. His session with JD had opened his eyes to the limitations of endorsements.

"Endorsements are mere surface acknowledgments—LinkedIn 'likes,'" JD had said. "Written recommendations, as they may be becoming extinct, are nuggets of branding gold. They'll enhance your credibility—especially when they're sincere and unsolicited—and point up the benefits of working with you."

"I'm sold," Gnik thought aloud. "How can I make this happen?"

He flipped open the laptop and soon was scrolling through his list of his connections, among them Pam and Garrett, who had helped him a great deal after he moved to the city. They were indeed mentors.

The next move quickly became apparent to Gnik: give recommendations to those in his network who had made a crucial difference for him.

These recommendations would be an act of gratitude rather than a ploy to secure recommendations for himself. *The latter is just selfish and misses the point of giving.*

He brought up Pam's profile, scrolled down to the Recommendations section, clicked on the link to write a recommendation, and stared at the empty box on the screen. And stared some more. Filling that box with something fitting—something *worthy* of Pam—seemed daunting at first. But Gnik knew that the best way to overcome his writer's block was just to write. He asked himself, "*What should people know about Pam?*" and began to type.

> Pam is the rare combination of mentor, accountability partner, savvy businesswoman, and friend.
>
> I first met Pam in a coffee shop just after I moved to a new city. She was knowledgeable, and easy to talk to, and became a trusted adviser almost immediately. I found her ability to ask insightful questions refreshing and challenging. She has taught me more than anyone about business relationships.
>
> Pam has earned my respect and admiration, and my highest recommendation. She would be an asset to anyone she does business with.

Gnik finished by customizing a notification message that LinkedIn would send to Pam and likely encourage her to return the favor. *But that's not why I did it,* Gnik reminded himself. *Giving is its own reward.*

He repeated the process on Garrett's profile page.

> Garrett is an uncommon executive. He is insightful, direct, and accessible. He's never too busy to point me in the right direction.
>
> His kindness is remarkable. He immediately connected with me and has been available to help me whenever I've asked. Each time we talk, he teaches me something new—just enough to keep me wanting more, but not so much that I have too much to digest.
>
> I have great respect for Garrett, and recommend him unconditionally.

Gnik sent it off with a custom message to Garrett, thanking him again for taking the time to be a "coach."

Maybe the reason people tend to skip making recommendations is that they require some time and thought, he mused. Then he went back through his notes from JD's seminar to see if there were additional insights to be gained.

JD had urged, "Go through your network and isolate the best candidates to write recommendations of you. Approach your satisfied clients, colleagues, strategic partners, and others who can vouch for your integrity and ability to provide services. Explain that you're in the process of expanding your reach on LinkedIn and tell them you'd appreciate a written recommendation. Let them know that even a few words from them would be valuable."

It's better to get a few well-written recommendations than a lot of them from people who just "phone it in." Recommendations are testimonials. Pieces of marketing. They are nuggets of gold.

Gnik went through his connections and made two lists. The first one included all of his First Degree connections for whom he felt comfortable writing a recommendation. There were a few college friends, some colleagues from his former job, and several people he had done business with in the city. *This isn't a big list, but it'll still take a bit of time to write the recommendations,* he thought. *Authenticity is important—I won't use boilerplate.*

His second list consisted of people who could vouch for his integrity and abilities. Looking at the lists side by side, he saw there was some overlap and eliminated the duplicates. Next, following JD's road map, he typed a message earmarked for each person he wanted to recommend.

> Because of our business relationship and friendship, you are someone I want to recommend on LinkedIn. In the coming days, I will write a recommendation for your profile, explaining why I believe other people should have the same confidence and trust in you that I have.
>
> If you are so inclined, and because you are someone I respect, I would appreciate it if you would write a note of recommendation for me, as well.
>
> Thank you for being a valuable part of my network.
>
> Gnik (With a "G")

Gnik sent the messages and checked the time. He'd spent a good part of the morning on LinkedIn. He remembered JD's final comments from the previous day's seminar: "You want recommendations from people of prestige. Executives. Thought leaders. People you have provided a service to. Excellent clients. The caliber is important. It's better to get a few, well-written recommendations than a lot from people who just 'phone it in.' They should be testimonials. Pieces of marketing in their own right. Nuggets of gold."

Gnik's Aha!

Recommendations have power when their language is genuine. I should ask trusted members of my network for thoughtful recommendations, and recommend them in return.

day 12

Explore the Power of LinkedIn

Gnik was up early to do some work on a marketing campaign for a new client and drew on the energy of a new morning to inspire the creative process. He left his apartment while it was still dark and walked to the coffee shop, where he grabbed a pastry and some caffeine. He sat in the familiar, molded-plastic chair and opened his laptop. Quickly engrossed in his project, he tuned out the flurry of activity around him.

By late morning, he nearly had completed the first draft of his campaign. After typing the final paragraph and saving the file, he shifted his attention to his social media efforts.

I had no idea of the power of LinkedIn. Curious about what more he could learn, he opened his internet browser and typed a search query:

Power of LinkedIn

The first link Gnik clicked on was powerformula.net, which brought up a page for an author and LinkedIn expert named Wayne Breitbarth. As Gnik browsed the site, he grew increasingly impressed with what Wayne had to say. *This guy seems to understand LinkedIn in a very different way.*

After reading a number of Wayne's blog posts and a linked article about him on forbes.com, Gnik was eager to speak with him in person. The website offered complete contact information including a phone number, which Gnik dialed. Wayne picked up on the third ring.

Gnik introduced himself and complimented Wayne on the resources he'd made available on his website, then asked, "In your opinion, what makes LinkedIn so powerful?"

"You're talking my language," Wayne said. "Most people think of LinkedIn primarily as a social media tool, like Facebook. But LinkedIn is really, at its simplest level, a database. It's the largest accessible database of professionals *for* professionals."

Gnik had never thought of LinkedIn as a *database*, but the minute Wayne uttered the word he knew that this seemingly simple idea was going to make a huge difference in how he used the resource.

Wayne continued. "When you look for something in any database, you search with keywords. When you're working on LinkedIn, you need to think about what keywords people will use when they're describing themselves."

"Describing themselves?" Gnik asked.

"What they do—their *meal ticket*. What words would you use to describe what you do?"

"Well, marketing, for one."

"Okay, but for someone who wants to find someone who does what you do, what words are they likely to search?"

Gnik thought about it for a second. "I'd say probably 'advertising,' 'promotion,' 'social media,' and 'public relations.' Obviously, I need to think carefully about the words people might use when they're looking for someone like me."

"Perfect," Wayne said. "Say you want to find a purchasing manager. You go to LinkedIn and search 'purchasing.' A list of names comes up. But what about all the people who have the same job function, but call it 'procurement?' And then there are those who do 'sourcing.'"

"They're all the same thing."

"Exactly. So, you need to be thinking about how people describe themselves. Those different words—the keywords—will be how most people find each other."

"I can use that in my own profile, too." The power of thinking of LinkedIn as a database was becoming clearer by the moment.

LinkedIn is essentially a database that professionals tap to learn about other professionals—with an eye toward generating new contacts and business.

"How else can I use the database?" Gnik asked Wayne.

"Let me show you one idea that can be incredibly helpful. Pull up any first-level connection."

Gnik quickly opened Pam's profile. "Okay, I have one."

"Now, look right below the profile picture ... click on 'Relationship.' Here, LinkedIn makes it easy to add reminders and notes. The things you add are visible only to you. I add a note if I learn any details about the person, like hobbies and interests. The reminder is a follow-up system—you can have LinkedIn notify you to take some action related to that connection. I don't know about you, but I connect with people all the time, and later I don't always remember how we met."

"I know what you mean," Gnik said. "With my network growing, I've been wondering how I can keep all my connections straight."

"Describe how and where you met," Wayne continued. "If you ever need a refresher, it's right there. LinkedIn also lets you categorize people with 'tags,' which are like file drawers. You can classify people as 'classmates,' 'colleagues,' or 'friends,' for example. Or you can create your own unique tags. This can be time-consuming, so be selective deciding which tags make the most sense for you. Maybe it's geography. Or client type. You could use trade associations ... any number of categories."

"I've used tags in other programs, so I understand the principle," Gnik said, "but I had no idea LinkedIn had the framework to categorize connections that way."

"It's a real plus," Wayne said. "You can pull lists of people with a common tag; that makes it easier to communicate with them. Finally, LinkedIn gives you a timeline of all your communication with each connection."

"Thanks for explaining that," Gnik said. "It's so much more powerful than I first thought. Is there anything else I should know?"

"There is one thing," Wayne said. "Are you aware that LinkedIn offers premium membership options?"

"I was offered a free trial subscription. Should I try it?"

"To tell you the truth, Gnik, for most people the basic LinkedIn account is fine. But to use this tool to its fullest potential you may want to upgrade. Why not check out the free trial?"

Gnik thanked Wayne for mentioning it and made a note to check out the premium options. Before they ended the call, Wayne said, "I want to leave you with this: Have you ever received an email saying someone has viewed your profile?"

"Absolutely," Gnik said. "I just delete them."

"I know something better to do with them, but that will have to wait for the next time."

The two men said their goodbyes, and, after a short break, Gnik got to work on his list of keywords.

Gnik's Aha!

LinkedIn is a powerful database that lets me target an audience through the use of keywords.

day 13

Interaction Brings Cooperation

Gnik was eager to learn what Wayne had in mind when he said he had a better idea for "profile view" emails than just deleting them. *I wonder what mistakes I'm making,* he wondered.

Before the morning snuck away from him, he sat at his kitchen table and opened his laptop. As he munched on a bagel with cream cheese, he typed into a search engine:

Business networking mistakes you must avoid

One of the top results took Gnik to a profile of author Ted Prodromou, who underscored three mistakes that people often make as they use LinkedIn to stimulate their business: 1) asking for the sale right after you connect; 2) focusing on yourself rather than the prospect; and 3) not following up on new connections.

Gnik shook his head at the idea of hitting a new LinkedIn connection with a sales pitch right off the bat, though he imagined plenty of people did just that. *I doubt it's a very effective approach.* As to the second mistake, Gnik felt he had become an effective networker largely by focusing on others. So far, his LinkedIn connection methods seemed to be closely patterning his personal networking strategies.

The third mistake in Ted Prodromou's list was particularly intriguing for Gnik. Since he'd begun actively networking with people offline, he'd made it a practice to follow up, solidifying several friendships in this manner. He had done some follow-up on LinkedIn, but not in any consistent way. There was something awkward about it, especially as he connected with people he hadn't met face to face.

Seeking a new way to engage, Gnik sent a connection request to Prodromou. Replacing the default connection message, he wrote:

> Ted, I read your LinkedIn article about three business networking mistakes to avoid. I was particularly interested in the third mistake—not following up. I'd love to hear your thoughts on how to engage better with connections, especially those I don't know personally.
>
> Thanks for your time,
> Gnik

He sent the connection request, then turned his attention to a news release he was working on for a client. After an intense but productive writing session, he left home for a change of atmosphere, finding a quiet corner in a cozy restaurant. While waiting for the sandwich he'd ordered, he turned on his tablet and checked email. He was surprised to see that Ted had not only accepted his connection request, he'd sent a personalized response.

> Gnik, thanks for connecting with me. I'd love to discuss ways to better engage with people you don't know personally. A few thoughts come to mind.
>
> Of course, I start out by thanking them for connecting with me.
>
> LinkedIn will help you know when someone's changed their profile, changed jobs, or had a birthday. Type a simple note and send it. That keeps you "top of mind."
>
> Be interested in people. I've found that when I do that consistently, more people find and look at my profile. That means I get more phone calls, more connection requests, and potentially more business opportunities.
>
> If I'm not on LinkedIn every day, my profile views drop. Fifteen or twenty minutes every morning is all it takes.
>
> So, think about your objective. Make daily goals and then go for them!
>
> Nice to meet you. I'd love to hear your thoughts.

So, first Wayne, now Ted, Gnik thought—each implying that profile views may be an important piece of the puzzle.

Gnik sat back and pondered the counsel he'd received in Ted's email. Opening the LinkedIn app on his tablet, he scrolled through his growing list of connections. *How many of these people haven't heard a word from me since we connected? Following up is just as important online as it is off.*

Just then the restaurant door opened and Gnik looked up to see a pair of customers entering. The two men looked back toward the dining room and waited for someone to seat them; when nobody showed, they exchanged a few words and walked out.

Gnik cringed on behalf of the restaurant owner. *That's two customers they just lost because no one was paying attention.* As the thought occurred to him, he recalled what Wayne had been talking about yesterday. *When someone looks at my profile—especially if it's someone I'm not connected with—it's as if he or she is walking into my business. They'll form an impression and either request to connect or not. If not, they're likely to walk out of my business and my life forever.*

Reaching out means more than just making a contact. Showing genuine interest will build your presence, as more and more people gravitate toward your persona online and, eventually, in person.

Gnik looked through his recently deleted messages, searching for those indicating his profile had been viewed. He spotted three, only one of which was from an existing connection. Of the other "viewers," one didn't seem to have anything in common with him, and he wondered how the guy had come across his profile. As he perused the second profile, however, he discovered a shared interest with Gina, who described herself as a social media marketer with Star Media.

Now what? he wondered, and the answer came immediately. *Thank her. Gratitude is an underused art—that's where I'll start.* Not quite ready to request a connection, Gnik typed a message:

> Hi Gina, and thank you for taking a look at my LinkedIn profile the other day. I see that, like me, you're involved in social media marketing. I wanted to give you the opportunity to ask me any questions that my profile didn't answer.
>
> If there's anything I can help you with, please let me know.

I never would have thought of reaching out to someone who merely viewed my profile, Gnik thought as he sent the message, *but it's a great way to reach out to someone who has shown some interest.*

He closed the cover on his tablet and paid the lunch bill. Pumped by his latest eureka moment, he walked briskly to his next appointment.

Gnik's Aha!

Following up with other users is a cornerstone of success on the LinkedIn network.

day 14

Maintain High Visibility

The morning sun was bright and the sky was clear as Gnik gazed with fresh eyes at the cityscape outside his window. Recalling his first conversation with Garrett about LinkedIn, he was amazed at the advances he'd made with his online network in just two weeks.

His thoughts moved through the lessons he'd learned in the previous few days, which had prompted him to reach out to people consistently, strengthening his connections. Then something dawned on him: He realized he hadn't looked at his group messages or posts for several days.

In customary fashion, Gnik took a seat at his kitchen table and opened his laptop. Scrolling through the groups, he found a post that looked interesting. When he clicked on the link, he noticed a section that listed the group's top contributors. The name of one,

Phil Gerbyshak, caught his eye. *Gerbyshak?* He brought up Phil's profile and noted his extensive list of accomplishments. He was surprised to see a cell phone number on the page.

"He's certainly making it easy for people to connect with him," Gnik said to himself.

The fact that Phil had written about publishing on LinkedIn encouraged Gnik to dial the number. Somehow, he wasn't surprised when Phil answered.

Gnik introduced himself and explained that he had been studying LinkedIn for the past couple of weeks. "I was looking through some group messages and noticed you're a top contributor. Your name caught my attention, and I was impressed with your most recent article about publishing on LinkedIn. I was hoping to pick your brain on becoming more visible—am I catching you at a good time?"

Phil thanked Gnik then jumped right into the topic. "When you are better known, you have access to more relevant people."

"What do you mean by *more relevant*?" Gnik queried.

"There are plenty of business-minded professionals who will hire you and can refer business to you. That's who you want to get in front of."

Gnik explained that he had joined several groups, but had largely held off on commenting on in-progress discussions. "Is that the best way to get in front of people?"

"Commenting on group conversations can certainly help," Phil said. "A good place to start, though, is to just post regular status updates."

"Why start there?"

"Well, first of all, in your status update you can talk about anything you want. New products or services you offer. Things you're doing. It's a way for your personal network to see what you've been up to. Groups don't want self-promotion, so you couldn't get away with having that kind of conversation in one of the group discussions."

"Okay," Gnik said. "Providing status updates for things that I'm doing, and confining comments on group discussions to the topic at hand. Is that the ticket?"

"That's right," Phil said. "Start with the status updates and get comfortable with posting something regularly. Your updates are posted on your homepage and are shared with your network. That's one way that you can stay in front of them. And you don't have to wait for a group discussion to match your interest or expertise."

"Makes sense to me," Gnik said, as ideas for strengthening and broadcasting his business began to fill his head. "I've been thinking about using my involvement in group discussions to increase my interaction with people in the group. Will my status updates have the same effect?"

"Absolutely," Phil said. "People can like your update, and they can comment on it or share it. When they do, your update gets shared with their network. So, your reach begins to extend beyond your own network. Your increased interaction with others gives increased visibility."

Gnik considered the implications of far-reaching influence throughout his network. "Does it ever go beyond connections sharing or liking one another's posts?"

"It can. LinkedIn also has a Publishing tool. It's a way to publish articles about your areas of expertise. It had been available only to 500 celebrity 'influencers'—big names you would probably recognize—but now they've opened it up to everyone. On your homepage, in the space where you would type your status update, click the pencil icon to open your access to the Publishing tool. You can write an article with pictures or video, and you can even include a call to action, such as inviting people to sign up for a newsletter."

"So a published article can have a larger reach?"

"It's impossible to know the potential visibility that you could reach with an article. Posts can be shared beyond your own network. And, when new people who want to connect with you view your profile, they'll see a link to your article post, including the image you used. On the other hand, people looking at your profile won't see a scrolling list of your status updates."

On LinkedIn, increased interaction will almost always generate increased visibility. That's the power of networking.

Gnik took a moment to digest this. "So, boiling it down, the most effective way for me to stay in front of my network—and others—is to post status updates, contribute to group discussions, and publish articles." He hesitated for a moment before adding, "That seems like a lot."

"You're not doing everything *every* day. Focus on updating your status at least a few times a week, but ideally a couple of times a day. Find any group discussions that you can add value to. Then, when you have something more to say, write an article. It's really not that overwhelming. With time and some consistency, you'll start to maintain good visibility in your network."

"I can do that," Gnik said confidently.

"And when you write an article, don't be afraid to share it with your relevant groups. Post a link to the article with some fresh comments with the benefits to group members. That's another way you can increase your visibility."

"That's a great idea," Gnik acknowledged with enthusiasm.

After they wrapped up their conversation, Gnik sent Phil a connection request. Then, armed with these latest insights, he posted his first status update.

Gnik's Aha!

By being visible, I can expand my reach to include people who are more relevant to my network. Increased interaction brings increased visibility.

day 15

Step Up and Out of Your Comfort Zone

It was Gnik's birthday, and he started the day with a hearty breakfast at a new local diner. *Happy birthday to me,* he thought as he glanced over the menu. He liked the fact that family and friends reached out to him on birthdays, but otherwise today was really no different from any other day. He placed his order and sat back to reflect on the blessings in his life, enjoying his anonymity in the unfamiliar restaurant as he looked out the window at the world in motion.

The buzz of his cell phone interrupted his reverie. *Probably a birthday text.* All morning, his phone had been delivering one greeting after another from his network of friends and associates. At this point he counted more than seventy birthday posts on Facebook along with a few LinkedIn messages. Several close friends had texted their best wishes. He responded to all of them appreciatively.

Ready to shift his focus from himself to others, Gnik left the diner on foot for appointment at a nearby non-profit organization. As he pocketed his cell phone, a call came through. He didn't recognize the number but answered anyway.

An unfamiliar voice greeted him. "Happy birthday, Gnik!"

"Thank you," he answered hesitantly, "Ahh ..."

The caller laughed. "You don't know who this is, do you?"

"I'm embarrassed to say I don't. I must not have your number stored."

"It's Phil—Phil Gerbyshak ...? We talked yesterday."

"Wow, *Phil*, I really appreciate the call—but how did you know it's my birthday?"

"After we connected yesterday, I looked through your profile. I saw that your birthday was today, so I set a reminder to give you a call." Phil chuckled. "See—you can't escape me!"

"Well, that was nice of you. Thanks for calling."

"Let me give you one more secret that we didn't talk about yesterday," Phil said. "Connections with people often begin with a 'Happy Birthday.' On my last birthday I got around 100 LinkedIn emails, ten phone calls, and six singing telegrams. Guess what I remember best?"

"The calls and the telegrams?" Gnik guessed.

Phil confirmed it, then shared the moral of his story. "Don't be satisfied with the default response. Be more human and add more interactions. Your friends will appreciate the effort."

They wrapped up the call and Gnik went into his meeting with the president of the non-profit agency. Following a productive meeting, he wrapped up a number of other projects before heading to his favorite coffee shop. It was now late in the afternoon, and he wanted to sit, think, and start to flesh out some article ideas that his talk with Phil yesterday had inspired. He sat down at the usual table, took out his tablet, and pulled up his LinkedIn profile.

Any online communication is better than none, but don't fall back on "rote" responses. Spend a little extra time and inject original thinking.

Just then Gnik's thoughts were interrupted by a familiar voice. "Happy birthday, Gnik with a 'G!'" Pam had entered the coffee shop. He was happy to see her, and eager to get her thoughts on the post he was planning.

After thanking her for the birthday wishes, he invited her to pull up a chair. "I have something I want to run by you," he said.

"What's on your mind, Gnik?" she smiled across the table.

He began by summarizing the things he'd been learning about and on LinkedIn, then shared his idea for an article. "When we first met, I had just moved here. I didn't know anyone and my networking skills were limited."

"I remember," Pam said with a wink.

Gnik flashed a knowing smile before continuing. "Well, since then, I've started my business and met a lot of great people. I've expanded my network, both online and off. But, really, I didn't realize how far I'd come until recently, when a friend told me he was impressed with my ability to connect with people. He said I have a way of putting them at ease."

"That's a great compliment," Pam acknowledged.

"It is, but what he told me next was what *really* surprised me. He said he wished he could be extroverted like I am. Like *I* am? I told him I've always considered myself an introvert."

Pam nodded. "Interesting." She motioned for him to continue.

"It has taken practice for me to get comfortable talking to people. I've realized that making a connection is all about the *other* person, and that's changed my perspective on networking. I used to think that you had to have an outgoing, magnetic personality to build and maintain a network, but now I realize that's not true."

"I agree. So what does that mean?"

"Well, I think people who tend to be introspective may not realize they don't have to alter their personality to attract others. I'm thinking of writing a LinkedIn article about it."

"That's a great idea, Gnik. You may not change the world, but you can certainly make a difference for the people in your network. I think you should do it."

Pam had to run, so Gnik thanked her and watched her through the window as she went to her car. The sun had begun to set as he opened a new document file and began to write.

The Introvert's Guide to Networking

"You're great at networking because you're outgoing. I'm an introvert—I can never be successful at it."

> My friend's confession was startling, only because he was speaking *to me*. He thinks *I'm* an extrovert!
>
> If you are more comfortable standing on the side-lines than being in the middle of the networking room, there's no reason to despair. Three things have helped me build and strengthen my personal network, even though I, too, am a wallflower at heart.

Gnik worked on the article until he was happy with it, then found an available online image of two people shaking hands—just what he was looking for. He posted the piece and emailed his introverted friend a link to it. He powered off his tablet, finished his coffee, and stood to stretch. *This has been a good day,* he thought as a smile crossed his lips. *A good* birthday, *to boot.*

As he walked slowly along the darkening city street toward home, Gnik was excited about the new momentum he sensed was about to come to his LinkedIn adventure.

Gnik's Aha!

Stepping out to publish can create unparalleled visibility with the people I'm connecting with.

day 16

Build Your Network Fast

Gnik put the finishing touches on two client campaigns and made some progress on a third before calling it a day. His buddy CJ had bought him a ticket to tonight's U2 concert for his birthday, and they arrived at the arena early.

During the opening act, Gnik went to the concession stand for something to drink. *Concerts are great places to people-watch,* he found himself thinking as he took in the scene.

"Big fan?" the man just behind him in line asked, making friendly chitchat.

"I am," Gnik said, "but this is the first time I'm hearing them live. How about you?"

"I've seen them several times," the man said. "You're in for a treat." Extending his hand, he introduced himself as Mike. The two shook hands as Gnik introduced himself. After they'd exchanged some rock and roll observances, the conversation took another direction.

"So what do you do, Gnik?" Mike asked.

Gnik gave a 47-second summary of his marketing business, wrapping up with, "I help people make the most of their marketing dollar. What about you?"

"I'm a consultant," Mike said. "I work with people on their social media strategies—especially on LinkedIn. Are you on LinkedIn?"

Gnik smiled. "If we'd had this conversation a couple of weeks ago I would've had to say no, but that's changed over the past two weeks. I'm starting to use it a lot."

Mike produced his smartphone. "Do you have the LinkedIn app?"

"I do, but I haven't used it on my cell. On my tablet, yes, but I generally find it easier to navigate LinkedIn on my laptop."

"True, but it's helpful on the fly," Mike said as he opened the app and started typing. "What's your last name, Gnik?"

Gnik gave him the complete spelling of his unusual name, and Mike quickly found his profile. Because they didn't have any common connections, he used Gnik's email address to send a connection request.

Gnik pulled out his own smartphone, opened the LinkedIn app, and saw the connection request.

> Gnik, I'm standing next to you in line to get a beer. I would love to connect with you on LinkedIn and talk social media strategies.
>
> Mike O'Neil

As he accepted the request, Gnik asked, "How do you use LinkedIn?"

Mike pointed to a small group standing around the T-shirt stand. "LinkedIn is a tool that lets me segment the people in my network, like that T-shirt guy."

Gnik grinned. "Can you elaborate a bit?"

"Well, look around. There's a cluster of people wearing the same T-shirt. Here, there's a cluster of people waiting to get a beer. Over there is a cluster of people who want a hot dog. We tend to group ourselves into clusters with something in common, whether it's a love for great music, food, fantasy football, or business needs."

"I never thought of it that way," Gnik said.

"We all instinctively work to build out and manage our own clusters," Mike added. "We associate with people who have common interests."

We're all members of several clusters. LinkedIn lets us find new people to join our clusters and new clusters for us to join.

Reaching the front of the line, Gnik put in his order and promised Mike they would talk later. Returning to his seat, he told CJ about his and Mike's interaction. Then U2 opened their first set and the two lost themselves in the music.

Several songs in, Gnik felt his phone vibrate. It was a LinkedIn message from Mike:

Beautiful Day is my favorite U2 tune. You?

Gnik typed a reply:

With or Without You. Where's your seat?

As Mike fixed his location, Gnik realized that he and CJ had the better seats. Since the concert was an hour old and there was an open seat next to CJ's, he invited Mike to join them.

A few minutes later, Mike slipped into the open seat. "Thanks!" he mouthed. After the final encore, Gnik took advantage of the reduced decibel level to properly introduce CJ and Mike. They talked for awhile as the crowd began to thin out, and realized they had some common interests beyond just the music. Mike asked CJ if he was on LinkedIn, then opened the app on his phone, searched CJ's name, and found his profile. Selecting the menu on the profile screen, Mike chose the "Customize Invitation" option and typed a message to CJ.

"When you think about it, you see things like this on LinkedIn all the time," Mike said.

"Like what?" asked CJ.

"Gnik and I met by chance, and we hit it off because we both like rock music. I could have done this on LinkedIn, but it works in person, too. When I see Gnik's friends, I can see that there are some who might make good connections for me, as well. We may have some common interests. That's how you and I met, CJ—we have a common interest and a common friend."

Gnik smiled in realization. "I would have never thought of it that way, but you're right. I could be applying that same principle to my LinkedIn connections."

"Right," Mike said. "When you make a new connection, many times you can see *their* connections. There's a search box, and you can search for what you might have in common. Explore whether you want to connect with them."

"Great insight," Gnik said. "I'm going to give it a try."

The three men left the arena and said their goodbyes. Arriving home late after a long and busy day, Gnik plopped onto his bed, completely exhausted.

Gnik's Aha!

My connection with someone on LinkedIn is based on shared interests or activities. Where I have something in common with one of *his* or *her* connections, that's an opportunity to proactively reach out, connect, and expand my network.

day 17

Find the Right People

The sun was up and Gnik, though awake, lay in bed with his eyes closed. The U2 concert had been a blast, and meeting Mike was a bonus. Now he wanted to enjoy the stillness of the morning a bit longer. After a few minutes, he hopped out of bed and got into gear. He didn't have any work commitments today, but wanted to continue his daily practice of strengthening his LinkedIn network. He pulled up Mike's profile and typed a message.

> Mike,
> It was great meeting you last night. I feel like we've made an important business connection, because in addition to loving U2, we both appreciate the power of LinkedIn. I'd love to talk marketing with you sometime.
>
> Gnik

Looking over Mike's connections, Gnik saw several who were of particular interest. As he scanned their profiles he received notification of a new LinkedIn message. It was a reply from Mike.

> Hello Gnik,
>
> Thanks for the great seat at the concert. I'm glad to see you following up already. You know, when you meet someone, there's a "temperature" to the relationship. You need to act while there's still a fresh memory of the interaction. The quicker you are to follow up, the better the results.
>
> By the way, I have a couple of friends you'd like. I'll make an introduction soon.
>
> Rock on!
>
> Mike

The idea of a relationship "temperature" wasn't unfamiliar, and Gnik liked the analogy. He had learned the importance of timely follow-up with contacts when he was networking in person; he had more than a few business cards for people he could barely remember.

On Mike's profile page, Gnik added relationship reminders of how they met, then added Mike's birthday to his calendar and moved on to other members of his network. *When I connect with someone new, I'll update my notes and contact lists so I'm current and don't wind up with a backlog.* After updating the contact information for several recent connections, he got up to stretch his legs a bit.

When time passes after an initial connection is made, a relationship tends to cool. Following up sooner rather than later helps relationships thrive.

Coming back to LinkedIn with fresh eyes, Gnik noticed a word near the search box that he'd somehow missed before. "Advanced" was clearly a link to a higher-level search function. Intrigued, he clicked the word and viewed an array of new search options on his screen. The default was for an "Advanced People Search," but an "Advanced Job Search" was also available. He had friends who were looking for work, and, his curiosity piqued, he explored the job search options.

Gnik quickly recognized the power of a LinkedIn job search. A searcher could enter keywords, job titles, and even search for specific companies and geographic locations. Running a couple of experimental searches, he discovered that LinkedIn not only made it easy for him to view available jobs, but he could also see any connections he had to the employer or job poster.

Returning to the Advanced People Search, Gnik thought about the marketing presentation he'd be giving at an upcoming business conference. He entered the ZIP code of the conference center and, searching his connections, was delighted to see that a few of them lived or worked nearby. He sent personalized messages inviting them to attend his presentation and perhaps to get together socially while he was in the area.

Continuing his exploration, Gnik tried various keywords, titles, and relationship levels. *I wonder if I know any scuba diving vice presidents,* he thought amusedly and was surprised when several results came up within his Second and Third Degree networks and groups.

This will make it easy for me to identify people I want to meet and build a relationship with, Gnik thought. He spent a little more time experimenting with Advanced People Search, reviewing profiles and customizing connection requests for a handful of people whose backgrounds were clearly relevant to his work.

Checking his email, Gnik discovered that several people had been looking at his profile and three had sent connection requests. He thanked those who had viewed his profile then turned his attention to the incoming requests. He didn't recognize the names, but one person had referenced his recent post on networking for introverts.

> Gnik,
>
> Thanks for your article. Until I read it, I assumed that I was doomed to fail at networking because I'm a bit shy. If you are willing, I'd like to connect with you and join your network.
>
> Scott

Gnik immediately accepted the invitation to connect and sent a thank you to Scott.

The other two messages were identical boilerplate:

> Gnik R., I'd like to add you to my professional network on LinkedIn.

I have no idea who these people are, Gnik pondered. *It's easy enough just to click connect, but it would be nice to know* why *we should connect.* Still, not wanting to ignore the requests, he replied to each of them:

> Thank you so much for reaching out. I'm sorry to say that I can't remember how we know each other. Would you tell me a little bit about yourself and what you're hoping to achieve by connecting? I'm always happy to help.
>
> Thanks, and make it a great day!
>
> Gnik

As Gnik shut down and closed his laptop, the concept of LinkedIn as a powerful database felt more clear and compelling to him than ever. *As efficient as a cruise ship social director,* he mused. Pocketing his cell, he headed out to run some errands.

Gnik's Aha!

LinkedIn is a robust database that speeds up and deepens my search for people I need to meet.

day 18

Follow the Leaders

It was still dark out as Gnik pulled on a pair of sweatpants, laced up his running shoes, grabbed his duffel bag, and headed out the door. As the sun began to brighten the horizon, he walked briskly toward the gym and his early morning workout.

Throughout his aerobic workout, Gnik took advantage of the opportunity to think about life and business without the distraction of incoming calls, texts, and email messages. Today, he was feeling slightly overwhelmed by the many things he could be doing on LinkedIn. *How can I get it all done?* he wondered.

Later, as he dressed, he thought, *I've made a lot of progress, but I'm far from being an expert.* He had a few minutes before his breakfast meeting with a client, and arrived at the restaurant early. As he waited, he glanced at his inbox. There was a new message from Dave, the photographer.

Gnik,

I don't know if you'll remember me, but I'm the photographer who took your portrait a couple weeks ago. We talked a bit about LinkedIn, and I remember that you were trying to learn how to use it more effectively.

I have a friend, Viveka, who is doing a webinar today. I'm sure she'll share some tips that will help you.

I hope you can make the call.

Dave

Gnik added the webinar to his afternoon schedule moments before his client arrived at the restaurant. After returning home several hours later, he was tweaking a marketing campaign when his calendar notification beeped, reminding him of the webinar. He went to the website, the show began, and Viveka Von Rosen got right to it.

"There are some things that you should do every day. You should eat a good breakfast. You should exercise. And you should get on LinkedIn."

She continued. "It's proven that if you update LinkedIn regularly, you get more likes and more shares. That means you get more engagement with your network. That's a great stepping-off point for developing and continuing relationships."

Makes sense, Gnik thought, taking notes. *And the whole point of my using LinkedIn is to develop relationships.*

"But just like exercising, it isn't just going to happen, is it? You never make it to the gym if you go when you have 'extra time,' right? You need to put that on your schedule. You need to do that with your LinkedIn activities as well. Schedule time every day. Make it a habit."

When you update LinkedIn regularly you get more likes and shares. That means greater engagement with your network, which will foster developing relationships.

"There's no place like home," Viveka continued. "Start on the home page and look through status updates from your connections. Like, comment, or share the ones that resonate with you. That should only take a few minutes every day. Next, check your messages. There's an envelope icon at the top of your page. Read and respond to your messages. Keep up on your conversations with your network. You have potential clients waiting to connect with you, or someone may be sharing a group or something else that is relevant. Look for the opportunity to engage with your connections.

"Check your notifications—the flag icon at the top of your home page. You can see who has viewed your profile ... people who have endorsed you, or commented on the things you've commented on. Again, look for the opportunity to engage with people.

"There are a couple of reasons you want to know who is looking at your profile, so stay on top of that. If it's someone you know, use it as an opportunity to stay in touch. If it's a competitor, keep an eye on them. If it's a prospect, reach out to them. The best investment you can make in someone is your time."

Next she moved on to personal status updates. "To create opportunities to engage with other people, it's important to update your status every day, at a minimum. Maybe even twice a day. It's generally best to post your status updates when people are likely to be on LinkedIn—Monday through Friday, during business hours. You can do it yourself, but it may be easier to use a social media scheduler like Hootsuite."

Gnik knew he couldn't post updates during business hours every day, and he made a note to research social media schedulers.

Viveka shared a number of useful tips. "As you grow your network, it's important to use LinkedIn's tools to manage your connections. Use the tagging feature to segment your own connections into groupings that make sense for you. Set reminders to follow up with people, so you can stay in the top of their mind. Maybe on Mondays you reach out to one group, and on Tuesdays you write and publish an article. Wednesdays you spend a few minutes searching for ideal new connections, and so on. You don't have to do everything every single day. But you do need to make it a habit."

She ended the webinar by inviting every participant to connect with her. Gnik closed his laptop and leaned back in his "thinking chair" to review his notes. Next, he drafted a schedule of his daily LinkedIn activities, blocking out time each day to focus on strengthening and growing his network. He found that the act of listing his various to-do's alone made the time and effort to accomplish them seem more manageable.

He printed his schedule and posted it on the wall near his desk, directly beneath a framed quote by Lee Iacocca: "The discipline of writing something down is the first step toward making it happen."

Gnik's Aha!

Nurturing my network needs to become a habit; creating daily and weekly task lists and using LinkedIn tools will help me make that happen.

day 19

Practice the Habit

With renewed energy, Gnik quickly went through his normal morning routine. After breakfast, he powered up his laptop, checked his daily task list, and logged on to LinkedIn. *Let's see how long it takes me to get through today's list.*

Following Viveka's advice, he started on his LinkedIn homepage. He read through the status updates and came across a couple of articles that interested him. He opened them in new tabs to read later, when he wouldn't be distracted from his LinkedIn "focus time." He liked a couple of posts and shared one with his network.

A status update from Justin said, "I'm trying to help a friend find a job," and briefly described the type of work the person sought. Gnik commented on the post, wishing the job-seeker luck and asking for clarification on his employment goals.

Next he went to his LinkedIn inbox, where he had three messages. He responded to the first two and archived them to keep the history of the conversation. The third message was an invitation to attend a sales presentation conducted by a member of one of his groups. The subject didn't interest him, so he deleted the message.

He moved to his notifications, which included various comments on earlier posts and two notifications of endorsements for his skills. *Take advantage of the opportunity to engage.* He sent a quick message to the two people who had endorsed him to keep the relationships current.

Two others had viewed his profile. Gnik checked both profiles; one struck an immediate chord and he clicked the Connect button on her profile page.

> Carol,
>
> I'm impressed with your accomplishments. As a fellow marketing professional, I'd love to share some ideas.
>
> Gnik

Finally, he looked through his pending connection requests, which included one "open" request from someone he didn't recognize. As he read her profile, he could see how she might be a valuable connection. He accepted the request then sent a quick message thanking her for reaching out.

Gnik checked the time. Sixteen minutes had elapsed since he'd logged on to LinkedIn, and he'd completed his "core" daily tasks more quickly than expected. He moved on to his weekly list. His plan was to post status updates once or twice a day, but he wanted a social media program to schedule the posts to drip into his status feed at specific times.

After reading reviews of several social media management tools, Gnik decided to try Hootsuite, which Viveka had mentioned. This app would allow him to manage various social media accounts—including LinkedIn, Twitter, and Facebook—from a single dashboard. He set up his Hootsuite account and easily connected his LinkedIn account. He spent about half an hour writing updates, which included articles and videos he believed would engage his audience. He scheduled 10 posts to go out, two per day, at various times during normal business hours.

Once he'd finished the week's status updates, Gnik pulled up his schedule and blocked out some time a week later to post status updates for the following week. For efficiency's sake, he planned to bookmark any relevant articles or videos he discovered during the week.

His calendar still open, he blocked out additional time the upcoming week for reading and responding to group discussions. Another day, he would write and post an article. Lastly, he scheduled time to proactively pursue new connections.

Breaking up my weekly tasks makes both my LinkedIn and overall schedules more manageable.

Having wrapped up his LinkedIn tasks for the day and scheduled his activities for the rest of the week, Gnik left his apartment for a walk. He spent the afternoon calling on business owners and managers in search of new clients and projects. His morning energy carried him through the day.

Back home, he put on some music and enjoyed the stillness of the evening. After dinner, he checked his email. Justin's status message from this morning included a new comment from Gnik's friend, Parker. He hadn't realized that Parker and Justin knew each other. Intrigued, he read the message.

> Hello, Justin. My name is Parker Dalton. I worked with Gnik back in the day, and we've recently connected on LinkedIn. I'm a national recruiter for an automotive engineering company and will be happy to help your friend. If you'll have him send his resume to me, I'll pass it around.

So Justin and Parker don't *know each other,* Gnik realized. *It was my comment on Justin's post this morning that enabled the connection.* This example of how two people who were not directly connected could find a mutual benefit through LinkedIn was a pleasant surprise for him. *And I didn't really even do anything ... Just by taking an interest in a friend's post, a friend of his has a possible job lead.*

Having learned that a simple act of liking or sharing a status update can have a far-reaching impact, Gnik broadened his perspective on LinkedIn. *We are all potentially connected with each other, and those connections are much closer than they seem.*

Gnik's Aha!

By regularly engaging with my network, I can have a positive impact on people I don't even know.

day 20

Crack the LinkedIn Code

Gnik checked his messages first thing in the morning to catch up on any overnight alerts. Pam had sent him an early morning text.

> Good morning! Have you cracked the LinkedIn Code yet?

That's catchy. "The LinkedIn Code." Got to remember that one.

After hastily fixing a breakfast snack to eat on the go, Gnik loaded his backpack with the supplies he would need for the day and headed to his first appointment. Pam's reference to "the LinkedIn Code" was still stuck in his head, and he did a quick web search on his tablet as he waited in the reception area of his client's office. The search led him to the website of Melonie Dodaro, a social media expert in Canada with a book out entitled *The*

LinkedIn Code. He requested the cheat sheet offered on the site then powered off the device as he was summoned to his meeting.

Gnik had been working on campaigns for three different clients, and after his third meeting of the day, he took a break in a quiet restaurant where he could grab a bite and connect his tablet to Wi-Fi. After opening Melonie's cheat sheet he quickly realized that "LinkedIn Code" was an acronym, each letter a reminder of how users should exploit the network.

He studied the pages. Some of the ideas served to reinforce things he had learned over the past three weeks, but there were new ones as well. He finished his snack, left the restaurant, and went to the nearby park to enjoy the beautiful, clear afternoon. He sat on a bench and breathed deeply, remembering how he'd run into Pam here once when he was having a bad day, and how handily she'd improved his outlook. He decided to call her rather than respond to her text of that morning. She answered directly.

"Hi, Gnik. How's things?"

"You know, Pam, I think I've unraveled the mysterious LinkedIn Code."

She laughed. "Is there *really* a LinkedIn Code?"

"Have you heard of Melonie Dodaro?"

"The name sounds familiar."

"She maintains that LinkedIn is doubly powerful because of its Google indexing. You know—how when you Google someone's name, their LinkedIn profile will often show up near the top?"

"Okay, I've noticed that," she said, "but what's with the code?"

"It's an acronym. Are you ready? 'L' is for *Listen* to the language that your ideal client uses. Use that language in your profile and in the messages you send."

He continued. "The letter 'I' is for *Invest,* as in invest time to establish your personal brand, and 'N' refers to *Needs.* Your profile headline and summary must speak to the needs of your potential customers. Next comes—"

"Wait a minute, Gnik," Pam interrupted. "Are these *your* conclusions or Melonie Dodaro's?"

"I haven't read her book yet, but it's all right here in the cheat sheet ... So, 'K' is for *Keywords.* Use them throughout your profile to get a high ranking in search results. Use terms that people will tend to enter when they're searching for your particular expertise."

LinkedIn taps into the power of Google indexing. People will Google your name, and your LinkedIn profile will often show up.

He took a breath before going on. "Next, 'E' is for *Enhance* which refers to using multimedia, such as videos, PDFs, and MP3 files, and 'D' stands for *Develop* a lead generation campaign. Use a daily task list and make sure your messages help develop your relationships. Put this on autopilot as often as possible.

"The second 'I' is for *Initiate* new relationships. To do that effectively you'll need to personalize your connection requests and other communications. Don't settle for default boilerplate.

"The second 'N' is a reminder to *Nurture* your relationships. Send value-based messages ... Are you with me so far, Pam?"

"I'm all ears."

"Okay, we move on to 'Code,' where 'C' is for *Connect* regularly with prospects and value-based partners to build your network. Your ability to find and be found can be limited to the size of your network—First, Second, and Third Degree connections—as well as members of your groups.

"The 'O' is for *Offline*. Move conversations offline as a way to convert prospects to clients. 'D' reminds you to *Dedicate* time every day to LinkedIn, and be consistent in reaching out.

"And, finally, 'E' is for *Etiquette*. Follow best practices. Don't pitch people your products and services the instant you connect. Instead of going after the sale, focus on the relationship."

"So, now you know what the LinkedIn Code is," Pam said, "but have you cracked it yet?"

He thought for a moment before replying. "I'm getting there, Pam. There's still a lot to learn, but I think I understand the value of LinkedIn as part of my overall networking strategy. Just like with in-person networking, it's the relationship that's important. Shaking hands and passing out business cards won't do much to develop an offline relationship, and the online equivalent is 'collecting connections'—a rote process for lining up leads. It's not effective."

"You're right, Gnik," Pam said. "People do business with those they like and trust. *That*, to me, sounds like a relationship."

With LinkedIn, just as with in-person networking, it's the relationship that matters.

The two spent a few more minutes sharing LinkedIn tactics and strategies, and Pam was clearly impressed by what Gnik had learned and implemented in just three weeks.

"I'm hosting a gathering of wedding industry professionals tomorrow evening," she said. "We'll be sharing ideas on growing business through leads and referrals. I know it's *really* short notice, but would you be willing to spend twenty minutes sharing what you've learned about LinkedIn?"

"I'd be honored," Gnik said without hesitation.

The student had graduated to teacher. *And* he was thinking of ways he could strengthen his relationship with Pam.

Gnik's Aha!

By implementing and embracing the LinkedIn Code, my approach to building connections will be focused on developing relationships.

day 21

Bring it All Together

How can I condense everything I've learned over the past twenty-one days into a twenty-minute presentation? Gnik was starting to feel a little nervous about the talk he'd agreed to give Pam and her associates tonight. *Not to mention, the last presentation I did kind of fell flat.* Thinking back to meeting Whitney three weeks earlier, he wished he had her talent for making people laugh.

Hoping to find some inspiration on LinkedIn, he sat at his desk and went through his daily task list. He engaged with a few of his connections, congratulating them on work anniversaries and job changes. Then he posted a status update.

> I'm going to be speaking to a group of friends tonight about how they can make more effective use of LinkedIn in their business. Do you have any great tips to share?

Because he had so little time to talk, Gnik decided that his approach would be to highlight his most important LinkedIn lessons. He placed a stack of blank index cards on the desk, headlined the topics he wanted to touch on, then added concise summaries for each.

Two hours later, his preparation was nearly complete and departure time was nearing. Hopeful to find a few helpful ideas via comments to his status update, he opened his profile page once more. Six of his connections had commented along with two people he didn't know. He printed the pages and hurried to the restaurant where the meeting was being held, arriving with about ten minutes to spare.

As he came through the door, Pam greeted him with a warm smile and an embrace. "I really appreciate this, Gnik. Are you ready to roll?"

"I'm psyched, but I'm also a little nervous."

"You'll do fine. Be yourself and share what you've learned. Looks like we have about a dozen people, and as far as they're concerned, you're the expert—you know so much more about LinkedIn than they do at this point. Just let them know what they need to do next."

Before the meeting began, Gnik walked around the room, introducing himself to those in attendance. He asked several of them what they'd like to know about LinkedIn, and made a mental list of specific interest areas. When Pam started the meeting, the murmur of conversation faded. Everyone found a seat and she announced the agenda.

"My friend Gnik Rowten is an amazing networker who has been studying the use of online tools to enhance one's business network. On very short notice I invited Gnik to talk to us about LinkedIn, and he was gracious enough to accept. I'm sure you'll appreciate what he has to say, and that he'll be willing to answer any questions you may have." With that, she turned the meeting over to Gnik.

"I'm very excited to be here," were the first words out of his mouth. "I can hardly wait to hear what I have to say." That drew a round of laughter.

He began by encouraging anyone who hadn't yet set up a LinkedIn account to do so immediately. "Your profile is the first thing to work on. It doesn't have to be perfect, but take some time to make it an accurate reflection of who you are, professionally and personally." He explained the value of creating a custom URL for your profile.

"Along with creating that great profile, you'll want to think early on about how you want to use LinkedIn. It's a powerful database that can help you reach potential business partners, prospects, employers, and employees. On the other hand, you can use it to stay in touch with people you already know and do business with. Neither is the right nor wrong way to use it—it's your decision and should be based on what works best for you."

Referring briefly to his index cards and the tips he'd received a few hours earlier, which he'd placed on the podium, Gnik spoke at some length about LinkedIn groups and group discussions. He explained the advantages of posting status updates, publishing articles, and liking and commenting on what your connections are doing and saying. His audience obviously grasped what he had to say about visibility, and the importance of engaging with others.

Gnik explained why LinkedIn's strengths as a database set it apart from other social media sites, and talked briefly about how to take advantage of LinkedIn tools. He told the group that LinkedIn could help them develop and deepen mutually supportive relationships, some of which would become important and even long lasting.

"LinkedIn will give you opportunities to engage with a wide spectrum of people. You may be notified of their birthdays, work anniversaries, and job changes. You'll get emails telling you when someone has viewed your profile. You'll receive notices when your status updates, articles, and group discussions have been commented on. All of these notifications are opportunities to engage more deeply."

"Take the conversation offline when you can," he added. "And, remember, it's all about the relationship."

As he wrapped up his prepared comments Gnik noticed a partially raised hand in the back of the room. "Yes? Question?"

"I've been worried about reaching out to people I don't know because I don't want to be penalized. Doesn't LinkedIn discourage connecting with people you don't know?"

"Good question," Gnik smiled, "and I'm glad you asked it. LinkedIn's official position is that you should connect only with people you know, because any *connection* will automatically have access to the primary email address on your account—that may be something you don't want.

"However, you won't get carted off to jail if you connect with someone you don't already know." There were a few laughs and then Gnik continued. "You may come across the term 'LION,' which is an acronym for LinkedIn Open Networker. It's an unofficial group that LinkedIn doesn't endorse because its members set out to connect with anyone and *everyone*. Whatever way you decide to go on this, you should have a personal strategy and stay true to it. And if you decide to reach out to people you haven't met and who don't know you from Adam, look for clues that they might be willing to connect."

Another hand went up. "For example?"

"For one, many people make it easy to connect with them. Their public profile may include an email address or even a phone number. Some will clearly state that they're open to connecting. See what you can glean from a user's profile, then decide what's appropriate."

LinkedIn helps you learn of your connections' work anniversaries and job changes, and lets you know when people show interest in your profile, status updates, articles, and group discussions. These are all opportunities for engagement.

Gnik fielded a handful of additional questions, and, by the end of his presentation, realized how much he had learned and implemented in just a few short weeks. He ended by again inviting people to connect with him, and emphasizing that the development of an online network requires an ongoing commitment of time.

"I'm no expert—just a regular guy trying to grow his network," he said. "If I can do it, so can you." He left the podium to an enthusiastic round of applause.

Pam walked to the front and thanked Gnik for making the time to speak to the group on such short notice. "I certainly learned a lot," she said to her colleagues. "I'm going to take Gnik's advice and do a better job making LinkedIn a part of my daily routine."

When Gnik arrived home, he posted an update to his morning status.

> Thanks for supporting and reinforcing what I've been learning about using LinkedIn. Tonight's presentation was a winner.

Gnik's Aha!

Success on LinkedIn requires dedication. Anyone willing to devote his time and energy can make the network a vital part of his business.

Epilogue

Gnik checked off the last item on his daily LinkedIn task list and looked at his work schedule. In a couple of hours, his first meeting of the day would begin. He settled into his chair and thought back to the start of his LinkedIn adventure less than two months earlier.

It had been just three weeks since he'd spoken to Pam's group, and he'd received several calls and emails from people looking for LinkedIn advice as a result. A lot can happen in three weeks, he thought, noting that virtually *everything* he knew about LinkedIn had come over the course of three weeks.

Thinking back to the day he'd met Whitney on the plane, he felt a deep sense of gratitude. *If we hadn't met, I'm not sure I'd know what I do about LinkedIn.* He picked up the phone and called her.

"Hi, Whitney, it's Gnik. With a 'G?' We met on a flight about six weeks ago."

"Hey, Gnik! Are you ready to talk about how to liven up your presentations?"

Good memory.

He laughed. "Maybe later. I actually did a presentation a few weeks ago, and it went well. I'm calling to thank you."

"Thank me? For what?"

"You got me curious about LinkedIn, and as a result I've connected with some incredible people and made some great friends. So, thank you."

Gnik enjoyed the fact that Whitney seemed a little flustered. She didn't have the time now, so he asked if he could call again soon to talk presentation technique. She said she'd be delighted.

Next, Gnik's thoughts shifted to Garrett, who'd been equally responsible for helping him see the way forward. He called his number.

"Garrett, it's Gnik. I just wanted to thank you for pushing me to learn about LinkedIn. Your questions caused me to think more deeply about myself, and how I wanted to use the site, and thanks to you my networking strategy has come a long way."

Gnik shared some of the highlights of his "education" with Garrett, who chuckled. "Sounds like you've been on quite a journey, Gnik. Now ... are you ready for the bad news?"

"*Bad* news? What do you mean?"

"LinkedIn is a dynamic social site and database. Things are changing all the time. Some features will be added and enhanced. Others may be discontinued. Your continued success will depend on your keeping up with the changes."

"I suppose you have some suggestions on how to do that," Gnik asked rhetorically.

"For one, LinkedIn has a blog that's a terrific resource for keeping up with insights and information. I subscribe to the updates, so I get emails sent to my inbox. It's an easy way to stay informed."

"Thanks for the tip," Gnik said, and wrote a note reminding himself to check out the blog.

After hanging up with Garrett, Gnik thought about the support he'd received from other people who'd known a great deal more about LinkedIn than he had at the outset. Everyone he'd contacted had been helpful and gracious, and he felt compelled to say thanks. He started by drafting a message to Donna Serdula.

> Dear Donna,
>
> I was realizing today the deep impact you had on my LinkedIn education. When I was young and naïve—that was just a few weeks ago!—you were kind and helpful as you answered my questions. I was surprised you even took my call.
>
> The help you gave me on my profile has been tremendously valuable. Thank you so much for your guidance.

Gnik wrote similar messages to several other people who had been instrumental in his progress. Finally, he had to thank Pam. He picked up his phone and called her.

"Thanks for taking a chance and asking me to speak to your group," he said after they'd exchanged hellos. "That presentation made me realize how far I'd come, and you're a wonderful mentor."

Pam smiled at the compliment. She was glad that Gnik couldn't see her blushing slightly. "That talk really made a difference for you?"

"No question," he said firmly. "And the thing is, you've had impeccable timing from the first moment we met. You seem to know the right questions to ask and just when to ask them. I really appreciate everything you've done."

"It's been a pleasure, Gnik," she said, smiling at his unabashed enthusiasm. "I always enjoy our interactions." She paused for a moment to gather her thoughts, then said, "I do have one question for you."

"Sure, Pam—what is it you want to know?"

"Well, now that you've become such an amazing networker—online and off—what's next for Gnik Rowten?"

"You'll just have to wait and see, Pam," he said without missing a beat. "*We'll* just have to wait and see!"

Gnik's 21 Aha! Moments

We hope Gnik's LinkedIn journey has given you a few ideas on how to make better use of LinkedIn. Gnik learned that it's not just what you know, but what you do with your knowledge. Implement the strategies. Reach out to people and connect with them. Spend time on LinkedIn and make it a habit.

We would love to connect with you on LinkedIn. Please let us know you read the book and share your thoughts with us. Meantime, for your convenience, Gnik's Aha! moments follow.

- Day 1: It takes more than just signing up for LinkedIn to be "linked in." I will need to learn LinkedIn and use it effectively if I expect it to pay dividends.

- Day 2: My profile may never be "perfect," but I should make it as complete as possible.

- Day 3: To be successful on LinkedIn I must be focused and purposeful. I need to know what it is I want to accomplish.
- Day 4: I don't need to know *everything* about LinkedIn. I only need to know what I need to know. Then, I need to put it into action.
- Day 5: My LinkedIn profile is like my business suit. It needs to show the world my values, my attitude, and who I am.
- Day 6: It's important to develop a rationale for how I connect on LinkedIn.
- Day 7: It makes sense to connect with people with whom I have an overlapping purpose or shared interest.
- Day 8: Joining relevant groups will accelerate my ability to add people with common interests to my network.
- Day 9: Groups give me access to people and give people access to me—even if we're not directly connected.
- Day 10: I want to make sure that LinkedIn endorsements on my behalf are consistent with my skills and expertise, and organized to my best advantage.
- Day 11: Recommendations have power when their language is genuine. I should ask trusted members of my network for thoughtful recommendations, and recommend them in return.
- Day 12: LinkedIn is a powerful database that lets me target an audience through the use of keywords.

- Day 13: Following up with other users is a cornerstone of success on the LinkedIn network.
- Day 14: By being visible, I can expand my reach to include people who are more relevant to my network. Increased interaction brings increased visibility.
- Day 15: Stepping out to publish can create unparalleled visibility with the people I'm connecting with.
- Day 16: My connection with someone on LinkedIn is based on shared interests or activities. Where I have something in common with one of *his* or *her* connections, that's an opportunity to proactively reach out, connect, and expand my network.
- Day 17: LinkedIn is a robust database that speeds up and deepens my search for people I need to meet.
- Day 18: Nurturing my network needs to become a habit; creating daily and weekly task lists and using LinkedIn tools will help me make that happen.
- Day 19: By regularly engaging with my network, I can have a positive impact on people I don't even know.
- Day 20: By implementing and embracing the LinkedIn Code, my approach to building connections will be focused on developing relationships.
- Day 21: Success on LinkedIn requires dedication. Anyone willing to devote his time and energy can make the network a vital part of his business.

Contributors

We couldn't have written this book without the assistance of the following individuals who know LinkedIn much better than we do. We are indebted to them for the time they spent with us, answering our questions and sharing their insights.

Jason Alba
jasonalba.com
inkedin.com/in/jasonalba

Wayne Breitbarth
Power Formula LLC
powerformula.net
linkedin.com/in/waynebreitbarth
twitter.com/WayneBreitbarth
(414) 313-7785

Melonie Dodaro
Top Dog Social Media
TopDogSocialMedia.com
info@TopDogSocialMedia.com
linkedin.com/in/MelonieDodaro

Phil Gerbyshak
Actiance, Inc.
phil@philgerbyshak.com
linkedin.com/in/philgerb
(414) 640-7445

JD Gershbein
Owlish Communications
owlishcommunications.com
jd@jdgershbein
linkedin.com/jdgershbein

Victoria Ipri
Learn Linkedin Fast
LearnLinkedinFast.com
linkedin.com/in/victoriaipri
(610) 908-5250

Mike O'Neil
Integrated Alliances
linkedin.com/in/mikeoneil

Ted Prodromou
Search Marketing Simplified
tedprodromou.com
help@tedprodromou.com
linkedin.com/in/tedprodromou

Donna Serdula
Vision Board Media
LinkedIn-Makeover.com
donna@LinkedIn-Makeover.com
linkedin.com/in/todonna
(215) 839-0008

Matt Scherer
Scherer Communications
mattscherer.org
linkedin.com/in/mattscherer

Viveka Von Rosen
Linked Into Business
linkedintobusiness.com
viveka@linkedintobusiness.com
linkedin.com/in/linkedinexpert
twitter.com/LinkedInExpert
youtube.com/LinkedInExpert
instagram.com/LinkedInExpert

About the Authors

Ron Sukenick is considered one of America's leading authorities on networking and business relationship strategies. He is the president and founder of The Relationship Strategies Institute, a global training and business development company that provides the business community with strategies for developing and effectively utilizing deeper professional relationships. He is a dynamic presenter, an intuitive business coach, an expert consultant, and a successful author. His presentations on relationship collaboration and transformation deliver practical information, humor, and immediate results.

Ron's work consistently focuses on the areas of personal and professional relationship success, and he has extensive insight into the processes that connect people. He shows his clients how to transcend standard networking practices to build more authentic and mutually beneficial relationships that enhance the bottom line. He has written about networking for more than 20 years as author, co-author, and contributing author in such books as:

- *Networking Your Way to Success* (Kendall Hunt, 1995)
- *The Power is in the Connection: Taking Your Personal and Professional Relationships to the Next Level* (self-published, 2004)
- *Masters of Networking* (Bard Press, 2000); a *New York Times* bestseller
- *21 Days to Success through Networking* (Information Today, Inc., 2013); an Amazon.com business bestseller

For more information, please contact Ron at rs@ronsukenick.com

Ken Williams is co-author with Ron Sukenick of the Amazon bestselling business book *21 Days to Success through Networking,* and author of *Irregardless* and *Marriage Advice to My Daughter.* He is an energetic speaker with a dynamic history of teaching, coaching, and training teams to achieve success. As a sales manager with Vector Marketing American Income Life Insurance, he recruited and trained sales agents, and learned the importance of creating and maintaining relationships.

Through his corporate work in customer service, sales, and human resources, Ken learned the importance of developing and growing mutually beneficial business relationships and associations. A forward-thinking professional, he has collaborated with business professionals in diverse organizations, offering his expertise in improving processes, training and mentoring, and improving customer service and relationships. He realized his passion for speaking and mentoring in 2008 when he joined Toastmasters, and he achieved the designation of Distinguished Toastmaster just three years later.

Ken is an exceptional communicator in both individual and group settings, and his services are much in-demand for business and creative writing. He currently offers presentations to schools, businesses, and associations. For more information, contact Ken at ken@thekenwilliams.com.